Relation-Ship

A Guide to Navigating an Enlightened Path

Natalie Marino

ISBN 979-8-9997714-1-4

Dedication

This book is dedicated to all my teachers and mentors, many of whom I have not personally met. To my children, who have been my inspiration to become a better human being; and to my loving husband, who has given me the strength and courage to write these words down and follow my dreams.

Preface

What Is Enlightenment?

In dictionaries,

Enlightenment is defined as "the action of enlightening or the state of being enlightened, particularly, having attained spiritual insight or knowledge."

In Buddhism,

It is the awareness that frees an individual from the cycle of rebirth, or samskara.

In life,

Enlightenment means letting go of attachments to situations, people, and things that are illusions. It is the release of blockages and stored impressions, and the recognition that changes in our perception arise from our inner source of oneness and peace.

By changing the way we look at things, the things we look at begin to change.

Enlightenment is beingness, a shift in awareness from fear to love.

What is real cannot be threatened.

Nothing unreal exists.

Herein lies the peace of God.

The quality of our lives is directly tied to the quality of our relationships. This sense of fulfillment stems from our ability to harmonize with others. Yet, before we can truly understand others, we must first build a relationship with ourselves, exploring and embracing the most intricate and profound aspects of who we are.

Table of Contents

Prologue

Relationships are the source of our greatest joy or the deepest grief in our lives. At times, we feel the urge to run away from them; at others, we search tirelessly for the right ones, often without success. The truth is, we live in a world of people, connections, and constant change. The only way to set our sails in the right direction is to learn how to navigate our relationships through these ever-shifting currents.

Relationships are a cornerstone of our personal and emotional well-being. They significantly impact our success or failure in every area of life—be it professional or personal. And it's not just about our relationships with others. In fact, I believe the relationship we have with ourselves holds even greater influence. It shapes how we relate to others, and vice versa. While we often assume that the thoughts, feelings, and behaviors of those around us affect us, the truth might be that it is our own behaviors that shape theirs.

Ultimately, strong relationships are essential to our health, happiness, and overall life satisfaction. It is through these connections that we find meaning, growth, and fulfillment.

To understand why we attract certain people and experiences into our lives, we must first explore where we come from. Human beings are remarkable. Our ability to communicate through language, to reason, and to remember is one of the many gifts that make us unique. Yet, the capacity for these traits varies among individuals. We differ in skin color, appearance, personality, ideas, and beliefs. So, no one-size-fits-all formula exists for how we form and maintain relationships.

We must get to know others on a deeper level—beyond surface identities like ethnicity or background. Only then can we build strong, healthy relationships. But from my experience, even before we attempt to understand others, we must first understand ourselves. Building a relationship with oneself is the foundation for connecting with others meaningfully.

When things go wrong in relationships, we often ask, "Why me? Why does this always happen to me?" At one point or another, we've all asked these questions:

- Who am I?
- Why am I here?

- Why do I keep attracting amazing—or sometimes disappointing—people into my life?

Through deep introspection, I developed a hypothesis that three core principles shape who we are today:

- We are wired for love—so let love in. Be willing to receive.
- The brain's primary job is to keep us safe and alive.

What we notice in others often reflects something within ourselves.

Thus, our thoughts and actions—rooted in our innate capacity for love and guided by the brain's instinct for safety—ultimately shape our destiny. In a way, we create our own fate. What you think becomes what you do. And your destiny is built upon your actions.

Thoughts = Words → Words = Beliefs → Beliefs = Actions → Actions = Habits → Habits = Reality → Reality = Destiny

You are an individual. Every person is different. Your relationships are molded by your uniqueness. You cannot copy someone else's relationship and expect it to work for you. Don't compare yourself to others. Instead, dig deep into your identity. Who are you? What experiences shaped you into the person you are today?

Explore your inner self. That is the first step toward understanding others and building meaningful, fulfilling relationships.

PART ONE: KNOW YOURSELF

Chapter 1: The Foundation of Self

The importance of knowing and understanding yourself is so profound that words often fall short. The immense value of self-awareness is illustrated by the fact that our entire lives are shaped by how we perceive and identify ourselves. How we see ourselves determines how we present ourselves to others, and others respond to what we project.

So, what does it truly mean to know yourself? What is self-awareness?

Self-awareness is the deep understanding of who you are, allowing you to build a solid sense of identity. This identity influences how we make decisions, navigate relationships, and shape our paths in life. Once we are empowered with self-awareness, we gain the ability to consciously steer the direction of our lives. But before we can truly know ourselves, we must ask: Where do we come from?

At birth, our families—whether parents, guardians, or other caregivers—lay the foundation for how we interpret and experience the world. We begin to form our personalities based on what they tell us about who we are. However, it's important to recognize that while our upbringing is deeply formative, it is only one piece of a larger puzzle. As we grow, our identity is shaped by a three-part framework: our personality, our beliefs, and our experiences. Understanding these components is essential to cultivating a deeper connection with ourselves and, ultimately, with others.

As young children, parents, teachers, and peers frequently compare us to family members. You might hear remarks like, "She's just like her mother," or "He has his father's intelligence." These comparisons reflect a natural human tendency to label and categorize as a way of making sense of the world. While genetics undoubtedly play a role, we must also recognize that we are each born with a unique energy—an innate essence—that influences how we initially respond to our surroundings. Over time, this energy matures biologically and evolves into what we call our personality.

This energy impacts not only our personal relationships but also our professional growth. Science has shown how people with a growth mindset approach their abilities differently than do those with a fixed mindset. Those with a fixed mindset often perceive their innate traits and energy as limitations. In contrast, individuals with a growth mindset see these qualities as foundations to build upon and expand.

In essence, our personality is a complex blend of inborn tendencies and the ways we adapt to our environment. For example, a naturally shy child may become more outgoing when raised in a nurturing, socially active household. Over time, this interplay between our core nature and the social influences around us shapes our personality, and as our personality takes shape, so does our sense of self.

Beliefs form another crucial layer of our identity. These are shaped by our thought patterns, often established during childhood. Beliefs extend beyond religion or culture; they include the internal messages we absorb about ourselves and the world. From a young age, we filter experiences through the lens of our developing beliefs. For instance, if a child is repeatedly told they're not good enough or not smart enough, they may internalize this narrative. Such beliefs can endure for years, deeply influencing self-perception, the goals we pursue, and how we connect with others.

Experiences, the third factor, are shaped by our past interactions and how we interpret those interactions through the lens of our beliefs. Our experiences are not merely events that happen to us. They are the stories we tell ourselves about what those events mean. Two people could go through the same experience, but based on their beliefs and personalities, they might interpret it in completely different ways. For instance, someone who believes they are resilient may view a setback as a learning opportunity. In contrast, a person who believes they are unlucky or destined to fail might see the same setback as confirmation of their perceived inadequacy.

Together, these three elements—personality, beliefs, and experiences—compose the narrative of our lives. This narrative shapes how we see the world, how we relate to others, and what we believe is possible for ourselves. Our subconscious mind is remarkably powerful in this regard; it clings to the story we've created and works tirelessly to maintain it as truth, even when that story no longer serves us. This is the essence of a self-fulfilling prophecy. For example, if we believe we are unworthy of love, we may unconsciously push people away or sabotage our relationships, thereby reinforcing the very belief we hold.

Sometimes, the stories we tell ourselves are empowering. If we've experienced love, support, and encouragement, we may come to believe we are capable, confident, and deserving of success. But other times, our internal narratives can limit us. Experiences of rejection, criticism, or neglect may foster beliefs that constrain our growth and prevent us from fully embracing the opportunities life offers.

This is why it is so vital to know yourself. When we take the time to reflect on our personality, beliefs, and experiences, we begin to unravel the narratives we've been living by—both those that empower us and those that hold us back. With this awareness, we can consciously choose which stories to keep and which to release. This process of self-awareness allows us to rewrite our narrative, aligning it with the person we wish to become and the life we truly want to lead. Understanding ourselves on a deeper level also provides greater clarity about the relationships we attract. Every relationship reflects some aspect of who we are—whether it's a strength, a vulnerability, or an unresolved wound. For instance, if we believe we are not worthy of love, we may find ourselves in relationships with people who reinforce that belief through neglect, emotional unavailability, or criticism. Conversely, when we nurture a strong, healthy relationship with ourselves, we begin to attract relationships that mirror our self-worth—ones that are nurturing, supportive, and respectful.

The way we respond to others is also rooted in our self-awareness. When we understand our emotional triggers and behavioral patterns, we can handle conflict or tension more mindfully, rather than reacting impulsively from a place of fear or pain. This emotional intelligence allows us to communicate more effectively, establish healthy boundaries, and navigate difficult situations with grace and resilience.

In essence, knowing yourself is the first step to creating the life and relationships you truly desire. It sets the course for our journey, allowing us to consciously steer our lives in the direction we choose. When we understand where we come from—our personality, beliefs, and experiences—we empower ourselves to make intentional choices, break free from limiting patterns, and embrace our full potential. Only then can we confidently and authentically navigate the "relation-ship" of life with purpose, clarity, and heart.

Chapter 2: The Subconscious Mind

The subconscious mind holds incredible power over our lives. However, in order to fully grasp this phenomenon, our minds must be deeply attuned, because the subconscious operates largely beneath the surface, beyond our conscious awareness.

Our subconscious stores beliefs, values, and ideas that shape our thoughts, actions, and decisions, often without us realizing it. From the moment we are born, the subconscious mind begins absorbing information from our environment: our family, culture, social experiences, and more. Over time, this accumulation of repeated experiences forms a self-concept that influences much of what we do. Understanding the subconscious mind is, therefore, essential in the journey of self-discovery. Though recognizing and acknowledging subconscious behavior can be challenging, doing so allows us to better understand why we think, feel, and act in certain ways, and how we can transform those patterns to improve our lives.

In essence, the subconscious mind is shaped by three fundamental factors: genetics, experiences, and personality. Each contributes to the formation of our self-concept—how we perceive ourselves in relation to the world.

Genetics provides us with intrinsic traits and tendencies, such as temperament, emotional sensitivity, or predispositions. Experiences then add layers of interpretation and meaning to those traits. Personality, which develops from the interaction of genetics and experiences, becomes the filter through which we interpret new events and relationships.

As we grow, the subconscious mind functions like a vast storage system. The life experiences it stores help categorize our likes and dislikes, fears and desires, hopes and limitations. For instance, if a child is consistently praised for academic achievements, the subconscious may form the belief, "I am smart and capable." In contrast, a child who is frequently criticized may develop the belief, "I am not good enough." These beliefs may not always be conscious, yet they shape our thoughts and emotions, and in turn influence our decisions. Over time, this process establishes a self-concept that can either empower or limit us, depending on what has been stored.

The mind continuously generates thoughts in response to its environment, storing them as experiences and beliefs. As we grow older, our reactions to situations are guided by what has been imprinted in the subconscious. It does not act solely on present circumstances; instead, it draws from past experiences to make sense of current events. This explains why we sometimes react intensely to certain situations without fully understanding why. Our subconscious is retrieving old memories, categorizing new events through that lens, and shaping our responses accordingly.

This automatic process enables us to navigate the world efficiently—but it can also trap us in repetitive patterns of thinking and behavior that no longer serve us.

Environment plays a critical role in shaping the subconscious through experience. The brain essentially becomes a record of its environment, and much of our thinking reflects the influences of the world around us. For example, if we grew up in a chaotic or stressful environment, our subconscious mind may be conditioned to expect chaos, even when it's not present. In such cases, we may unconsciously seek out or even create situations that reinforce the belief that the world is unpredictable or unsafe. This happens because the subconscious is programmed to maintain consistency between our internal beliefs and external reality.

A critical question arises: Does our environment control our thinking, or does our thinking control the environment? For most people, it's the former. We often allow our surroundings—our family, job, social circle, and even societal norms—to dictate how we think, feel, and act. When we do this, we essentially live on autopilot, reinforcing the same patterns over and over again. The environment shapes our thoughts, our thoughts shape our actions, and our actions ultimately shape our reality. This cycle can be difficult to break, especially when we're unaware of the role our subconscious mind plays in maintaining it.

However, it is possible to reverse this process. To create real change in our lives, we must learn to think beyond our environment. This requires becoming conscious of the subconscious patterns that influence our thinking. We must deliberately adopt new, more empowering ways of thinking. When we shift our internal dialogue and beliefs, we begin to influence our environment rather than letting it control us.

The challenge is that most of us define ourselves by our experiences, rather than seeing ourselves as the person who had those experiences. For instance, someone who has faced repeated failure may internalize the belief, "I am a failure," instead of recognizing that failure is merely something they experienced. This identification with our experiences creates a rigid self-concept that is hard to change. We become trapped by our past, replaying the same thoughts and behaviors because they feel familiar and safe, even if they're not beneficial.

To break free from this dynamic, we need to reframe how we understand ourselves. Rather than defining ourselves by what we've been through, we must see ourselves as capable of growing and learning from those experiences. This shift in perspective opens the door to new possibilities and frees us from the limitations of our subconscious programming.

One of the most powerful ways to transform the subconscious mind is by understanding the relationship between our thoughts, beliefs, and actions. It begins with the simple formula described above: Thoughts become words, words become beliefs, beliefs become actions, actions become habits, and habits become reality. In other words, our current reality is largely a reflection of our past thoughts and beliefs. If we want to change our reality, we must begin by changing our thoughts.

Let's break down the formula. When we repeatedly think a certain way, those thoughts become ingrained as beliefs. For example, if we constantly tell ourselves, "I'm not good enough," that thought eventually hardens into a belief that shapes how we act in the world. This belief might cause us to avoid challenges or overlook opportunities, leading to the very outcomes we fear. Our actions, driven by those beliefs, become habits: automatic behaviors we repeat with little conscious thought. Over time, these habits shape our reality, influencing our relationships, careers, and overall life experience.

The power of the subconscious mind lies in its ability to maintain these patterns. It doesn't distinguish between helpful and harmful beliefs; it simply preserves what it has stored. That's why changing long-held beliefs is so challenging. They are deeply embedded and reinforced by years of habitual thinking and behavior.We've established that our unconscious mind exerts a powerful influence over our lives, giving rise to deeply ingrained ideas, values, and assumptions that shape how we perceive the world and respond to it. These beliefs are not passive thoughts quietly residing in the background. They actively drive our perceptions, choices, and actions, affecting nearly every aspect of our daily experience, especially in building relationships. Understanding how these subconscious influences operate is essential for anyone seeking to take control of their life, relationships, and personal growth.

One of the key ways subconscious beliefs influence us is through perception: how we interpret and make sense of the world around us. Our perceptions act like filters, coloring the way we view everything from relationships to opportunities to challenges.

For example, someone with a subconscious belief that they are unworthy of love might interpret a friend's short reply as a sign of disinterest or rejection, even if the friend is simply busy or distracted. Conversely, a person with a strong sense of self-worth may remain unbothered by the same scenario, recognizing that other explanations are likely. In this way, subconscious beliefs shape our interpretations of others' actions, often reinforcing the beliefs we already hold.

Through a phenomenon known as confirmation bias, the brain is wired to seek out information that confirms what it already believes. This means that if you hold a belief, whether positive or negative, your subconscious mind will gravitate toward evidence that supports it. For instance, someone who believes they're not good enough might unconsciously focus on and remember their mistakes while overlooking their successes. This selective attention makes it difficult to adopt a more balanced perspective. Over time, it creates a self-reinforcing loop: subconscious beliefs shape perception, and those perceptions, in turn, strengthen the beliefs.

The influence of subconscious beliefs doesn't stop at perception. They also drive our actions. Our thoughts and beliefs form the mental blueprint for how we behave. If you believe you are capable and deserving, you're more likely to take bold actions and pursue opportunities. On the other hand, if you believe you're not good enough or destined to fail, you may avoid challenges, procrastinate, or even self-sabotage when opportunities arise. In many cases, our behaviors are direct reflections of our underlying beliefs, whether we're consciously aware of them or not.

A striking example of this dynamic can be seen in relationships. Imagine someone who holds the subconscious belief that they are unlovable, perhaps rooted in early childhood experiences where love was conditional or scarce. This belief might lead them to act in ways that sabotage their relationships: pushing others away, becoming overly critical, or tolerating toxic dynamics. In doing so, they unconsciously seek to validate their belief that love is unattainable. Their actions, shaped by this deep-seated belief, generate a reality in which fulfilling relationships are elusive, thereby reinforcing the belief that sparked those actions in the first place.

The cycle between subconscious beliefs, perceptions, and actions is difficult to break because it operates largely beneath our conscious awareness. These beliefs feel so familiar and automatic that we rarely question them. The good news, however, is that these influences are not fixed. With conscious awareness and deliberate effort, we can change our beliefs, and by doing so, transform the way we perceive and interact with the world.

To begin shifting these unconscious influences, it's important to recognize that we often define ourselves by our past experiences rather than as the person who lived through them. This distinction is crucial. We are not the sum of our failures, disappointments, or traumas. We are the individuals who endured those experiences and have the power to reshape how we understand them. By reframing our self-concept, we can start to challenge the subconscious beliefs that hold us back.

For instance, if you catch yourself thinking, "I'm not good enough," pause and reflect on where that belief originated. Was it internalized from a critical parent or teacher? Does it truly reflect who you are today, or is it simply a story you've been telling yourself for years? Once you identify the root of the belief, you can begin to rewrite it. Start by adopting new thoughts and beliefs that align with the person you want to become.

It's also helpful to remember that, while the brain is a record of our environment, we have the power to change that environment, both internally and externally. By deliberately exposing ourselves to new ideas, experiences, and people, we can challenge the outdated beliefs stored in our subconscious and create new, empowering patterns of thought. This process requires time and effort, but it is entirely possible.

One powerful phenomenon to understand is the self-fulfilling prophecy, where our beliefs shape our thoughts, which drive our actions, ultimately leading to results that confirm those initial beliefs. This cyclical process influences every area of our lives, often operating beneath our conscious awareness. It's like a loop: what we believe shapes how we think; how we think drives what we do; and what we do leads to outcomes that reinforce those beliefs. Once you understand this cycle, it becomes clear how much of your life is a reflection of the stories you tell yourself—and how changing those stories can transform your reality.

Think of it this way: your mind is like a garden, and your beliefs are the seeds. If you plant seeds of doubt, fear, or unworthiness, they will grow into thoughts and actions that reflect those beliefs. On the other hand, if you plant seeds of confidence, hope, and abundance, your thoughts and actions will create a reality that supports those positive beliefs. The cycle begins with the choice of seeds: your beliefs.

The Cycle Explained

It all starts with belief. Your beliefs generate your thoughts. A person who believes they aren't good enough might think, "I'm going to fail," "I'll never be able to do this," or "Other people are more capable than I am." These thoughts form a mental framework that guides how you interpret events and situations in your life. Over time, these thoughts shape your mindset, which then influences the actions you take.

The results of those actions then reinforce the original belief. If you believe you're going to fail and don't put in the necessary effort, chances are, you'll fall short—confirming your initial belief that you weren't good enough. And so the cycle repeats.

The same process applies to positive beliefs. If you believe in your ability to succeed, you're more likely to take decisive action, which leads to favorable outcomes that strengthen your original belief. This creates a cycle of confidence, momentum, and growth.

Negative beliefs often subconsciously lead to common fears and reservations, such as a persistent lack of self-confidence. These internal doubts stem from questioning our own worth and potential.

Let's explore a few examples that illustrate how this cycle plays out:

The Student Who Believes They're Bad at Math

Imagine a student who has internalized the belief that they are bad at math. Perhaps they struggled with the subject in the past, leading them to conclude they'll never be good at it. This belief fuels negative thoughts like, "Why even try? I'm just going to fail." These thoughts cause the student to put in less effort, avoid studying, or even skip class altogether. As a result, their performance declines, confirming the belief that they're bad at math. Over time, the student may give up entirely, convinced they lack the ability to succeed in the subject.

Now, imagine that same student begins to challenge the belief, thinking instead, "I can improve with practice." Their thoughts might shift to something more encouraging: "If I try harder and get help, I can get better." This new mindset leads to more effort: studying regularly, asking for help, and staying engaged in class. Eventually, their grades improve, reinforcing the new belief that they can succeed in math after all.

The Professional Who Believes They Are Incompetent

A professional who doubts their abilities at work might think, "I'm not good enough for this position," or "Sooner or later, everyone will realize I'm a fraud." These beliefs lead to thoughts such as, "I'll mess up this project," or "I'm not as capable as my coworkers." As a result, they might avoid new responsibilities or stay silent during meetings, afraid of making mistakes or appearing incompetent.

Because they hold back, they miss opportunities to showcase their skills and value. The lack of recognition or advancement at work reinforces their belief that they're not competent. This can trigger a downward spiral, where their hesitation and inaction lead to stagnation, in turn validating their original belief.

However, if this person were to start believing in their competence and worth, their inner dialogue would change. They might think, "I am good at what I do," and begin to contribute more confidently, take on new projects, and seek constructive feedback. These actions could result in greater success and acknowledgment, strengthening the belief that they are indeed capable.

The Person Who Believes They Are Unlovable

Now consider a more personal example: someone who believes they are unlovable—perhaps due to past experiences of rejection or emotional pain. This belief gives rise to thoughts like, "No one will ever truly love me," or "I'm not worthy of being loved." These thoughts may cause the person to act in ways that push others away: being overly defensive, emotionally distant, or even sabotaging relationships when they begin to feel close to someone.

As a result, they experience more rejection and isolation, reinforcing the belief that they are unlovable.

But their thoughts would shift if they were to challenge their belief and adopt a new mindset, such as, "I am worthy of love and connection." As a result of this, the belief would emerge, "I can build meaningful relationships." This new perspective might lead them to open up, engage more authentically, and pursue healthier connections. Over time, they would likely experience more fulfilling relationships, affirming their new belief that they are, in fact, lovable.

Another primal fear born from the belief cycle is the fear of abandonment. This fear can lead us to believe that unless we give everything in a relationship, the other person will leave. With this mindset, we may remain in unfulfilling or even harmful relationships simply because we're afraid: "If I let go, I'll end up alone forever." These thoughts create a sense of desperation, making us tolerate neglect, disrespect, or even abuse in the name of preserving the relationship.

Our actions—such as staying silent, ignoring red flags, or sacrificing our own needs—reinforce these beliefs. As we lose ourselves in the relationship, our sense of self-worth diminishes further. And if the relationship ends despite all our efforts, the fear of abandonment feels confirmed.

Imagine someone in a relationship who is afraid to say no to their partner, tolerating abuse and clinging to the relationship out of fear that being alone would be worse. Now imagine that same individual challenges this belief, thinking instead: "I deserve a relationship that serves me as much as I serve it." This shift in mindset could inspire them to communicate boundaries, prioritize self-care, or even walk away from an unhealthy dynamic. Over time, they would likely attract relationships built on mutual respect and love. This breaks the cycle and gives rise to a healthier belief: that it's okay to end a relationship with the wrong person, and that our happiness and self-worth do not depend on someone else.

Trust is another challenge rooted in limiting beliefs: an uncertainty that causes us to hesitate before committing, due to the fear that things will fall apart. For example, someone who struggles to trust might think, "What if I commit and they leave me?" or, "What if I open up and get hurt?" These thoughts create hesitation, leading the person to hold back emotionally, avoid vulnerability, or stay partially disengaged even in promising relationships.

But what if that person adopted a new belief, such as: "While nothing in life is certain, connection is worth the risk"? Their thoughts might shift to: "I'll take it one step at a time," or, "Even if this doesn't work out, I'll grow from the experience." This mindset encourages open communication, acceptance of uncertainty, and the release of assumptions and self-imposed negative expectations.

While the self-fulfilling prophecy can trap us in cycles of limiting beliefs and undesirable outcomes, it is entirely possible to break free and create a new cycle of positive change. The first step is becoming aware of the beliefs driving your thoughts and behaviors. Ask yourself: "What do I believe about myself in this area of my life? Are these beliefs helping me—or holding me back?"

Once you identify a limiting belief, challenge it. Ask: "Is this belief based on my past, or does it accurately reflect who I am now?" Often, we carry outdated beliefs from childhood or past failures into the present, even when they no longer serve us. By questioning these beliefs and replacing them with more empowering ones, you can shift the cycle in your favor.

As you adopt new, empowering beliefs, you'll notice changes in your thoughts. This internal shift leads to new actions—more proactive, confident, and aligned with your goals. And as your actions evolve, so will your results, reinforcing your new beliefs. In this way, the self-fulfilling prophecy can become a powerful tool for growth and transformation, rather than a trap that holds you back.

The self-fulfilling prophecy is a cycle that begins with our beliefs and ends with the results we experience in life. By understanding and interrupting this cycle—by taking control of our beliefs—we can free ourselves from limiting patterns and create a life that aligns with our true potential.

Chapter 3: The Brain's Role

The brain is often described as a sophisticated biological computer, but it is far more than that. It not only processes information but also serves as an intricate storage system, cataloging the entirety of our experiences, thoughts, emotions, and memories. The way it records and processes this information shapes the core of who we are, influencing how we interact with the world, make decisions, and form our identity. In essence, our brain holds the story of our lives. Yet, unlike a simple recording device, it continually filters, interprets, and modifies the information it receives.

When we speak of the brain as a record, we refer to its role in capturing and storing experiences from the moment we are born. These experiences come in many forms. Some are sensory inputs such as sights, sounds, and smells, while others are emotional or cognitive responses to the situations we encounter. All of these elements are logged in our brains, often unconsciously. We may not actively recall the countless details we experience each day, but our brain meticulously registers them, often determining future responses based on these internal records.

One of the most fascinating aspects of the brain is its ability to process new information by comparing it to what is already stored. This function enables us to navigate complex environments without constantly having to learn everything from scratch. For instance, when you enter a room and see a chair, your brain immediately recalls past experiences with chairs, allowing you to understand its purpose without conscious effort. This continuous comparison between past and present underpins much of our understanding of the world.

But the brain doesn't just record practical, everyday objects. It also stores our emotional and relational experiences in ways that deeply influence our sense of self and behavior. A child raised in a loving, supportive environment may develop neural pathways that associate certain behaviors or interactions with safety and trust. In contrast, someone who experienced trauma or neglect may have a brain wired to recognize danger or distrust. These internal records often operate below the level of conscious awareness, yet they subtly shape how we interpret new experiences and form relationships.

Importantly, the brain doesn't simply capture what happens to us—it also assigns meaning to it. This is where its processing function becomes essential. Information is not stored as neutral data but is colored by our emotional responses, beliefs, and interpretations at the time of the event. Two people may live through the same situation, but their brains can encode and process it in completely different ways based on their prior experiences and mental frameworks. This highly individualized recording system is what makes each person's perspective unique.

A core function of the brain in all of this is to keep us safe. This survival instinct means the brain gives greater attention and priority to experiences it perceives as threatening or dangerous. Such experiences are logged with heightened detail, ensuring we are better equipped to avoid similar threats in the future. This is why negative memories—especially those related to fear or trauma—often feel more vivid and long-lasting than positive ones. The brain's primary goal is survival, so it stores these events as warning signals to protect us.

To ensure our safety, the brain may also prevent us from engaging in new experiences, making changes, or taking chances due to a fear of the unknown or because such experiences are unfamiliar. The brain is wired to favor what is familiar, as familiarity provides a sense of safety, even if that familiarity is ultimately unhealthy or unfulfilling. As a result, anything foreign or unfamiliar is often perceived as a potential threat, leading to hesitation and resistance. This built-in mechanism keeps us rooted in the status quo even when personal growth or better opportunities await, making it difficult to step outside our comfort zones.

However, this survival-driven recording system can sometimes backfire. When the brain becomes overly focused on cataloging negative experiences, it can create a biased view of the world. Imagine someone who grew up in an environment where they were frequently criticized. In an effort to protect them, their brain might store those memories in a way that leads them to expect criticism from others even when it isn't present. Alternatively, they might develop a tendency to over-criticize others in a way that becomes destructive to relationships. Over time, this pattern can shape their self-concept, causing them to feel insecure, doubt themselves even in safe situations, or become excessively critical of others.

The brain's ability to store information as a record isn't limited to past events. It also influences how we anticipate the future. This happens because the brain draws on previous experiences to predict what might happen next. If you've experienced success in a particular type of situation, your brain will store that memory and use it to encourage you to engage in similar experiences again. Conversely, if you've encountered failure or rejection, your brain may steer you away from similar situations, even when the circumstances have changed. In this way, the brain functions as both a record keeper and a guide, shaping future decisions based on past experiences.

One of the brain's most powerful tools in this recording process is neuroplasticity, the ability to change and adapt in response to new experiences. While the brain is constantly recording and processing information, it is not fixed or static. This means even deeply ingrained thought patterns or behaviors can be changed with sufficient new input. Neuroplasticity gives us the capacity to reshape how the brain stores and processes information, allowing us to update outdated habits or beliefs. For instance, someone who has always responded to stress with anxiety can, over time, train their brain to react with calmness or focus instead.

However, this process of rewiring the brain doesn't occur automatically. It requires conscious effort and repeated practice. The brain's default mode is to rely on past records because it is more efficient. Changing that pattern means intentionally exposing the brain to new experiences that challenge the old narrative. For example, if you've always believed you're not good at public speaking because of one bad experience, your brain will likely store that belief as fact. But by practicing consistently and embracing new speaking opportunities, you can create new neural records that eventually override the old ones.

At the core of the brain's functioning is its relentless drive to ensure survival. While the external world has evolved dramatically, the brain still operates according to fundamental principles that have guided it for millennia: safety, connection, and bonding. These instincts are deeply rooted in our biology and shape the way we relate to ourselves and others. In the realm of relationships, these survival instincts play an especially powerful role, guiding our behaviors, choices, and reactions, often at a subconscious level.

From an evolutionary standpoint, our ancestors depended heavily on the brain's focus on survival. Early humans lived in environments filled with physical threats: predators, harsh weather, and scarce resources. The brain evolved to detect and respond to danger quickly and efficiently. Today, although most of us no longer face daily life-and-death threats, the brain continues to prioritize safety above all else. The dangers we now encounter are more psychological or emotional than physical, but the brain's survival mechanisms remain largely the same.

In relationships, this focus on safety can manifest in various ways. For instance, when we meet new people, our brain quickly assesses whether they are trustworthy or pose a potential threat. This is often referred to as a "gut instinct" or intuition. In reality, the brain is drawing on past experiences, interpreting body language cues, and analyzing subconscious signals to make a snap judgment. While these judgments aren't always accurate, they are the brain's way of protecting us from potential harm.

This instinct for safety is closely linked to our need for connection. Human beings are inherently social creatures, and our survival has always depended on our ability to form strong bonds with others. Early humans relied on their tribes or social groups for protection, food, and shared responsibilities. Being part of a group increased the chances of survival, which is why the brain developed mechanisms to encourage social bonding. This drive for connection is not just about physical survival, it also supports emotional and psychological well-being.

In today's world, the brain's focus on connection continues to shape how we navigate relationships. Whether it's a romantic partner, family member, friend, or colleague, the bonds we form are central to our sense of safety and stability. When we feel securely attached to someone, the brain registers that relationship as a source of comfort and reassurance. This is why positive relationships can have such a profound impact on our mental and emotional health. Conversely, when relationships are unstable or filled with conflict, the brain interprets this as a threat to our well-being.

This survival-driven need for connection is most evident in how the brain responds to attachment. The attachment system, which develops in early childhood, is designed to ensure we form strong, reliable bonds with caregivers. As infants, our survival depended on caregivers for nourishment, warmth, and protection. The brain's wiring during this critical period plays a crucial role in shaping future relationships. Children who receive consistent, nurturing care typically develop secure attachment styles, which form the basis for healthy connections later in life. In contrast, children who experience neglect, inconsistency, or trauma may develop insecure attachment styles, leading to difficulties in forming and maintaining relationships as adults.

The brain's emphasis on safety and bonding is also evident in how we respond to conflict or emotional distress in relationships. When we feel threatened physically, emotionally, or relationally, the brain activates the fight-or-flight response. This instinctive reaction prepares the body to either confront the danger or escape from it. In the context of relationships, this might manifest as arguing with a partner, distancing oneself from a friend, or emotionally withdrawing when hurt. While the fight-or-flight response can be helpful in situations of actual danger, it may cause problems in relationships when we react too quickly or defensively to perceived threats that aren't as severe as our brain believes.

Another common response is the freeze response. This reaction causes us to avoid addressing the issue, sweeping things under the rug and pretending nothing has changed. In reality, the problem remains, just temporarily hidden. While denial or avoidance might offer short-term relief, unresolved issues often grow over time. Left unaddressed, these problems can resurface later as more serious threats to the connection.

However, it's not just conflict that triggers survival instincts. The brain is also wired to seek connection and bonding as a means of ensuring safety. Oxytocin, often referred to as the "love hormone," is released during physical touch, intimacy, and even social bonding. This hormone plays a vital role in fostering feelings of trust, security, and closeness in relationships. It's the brain's way of encouraging us to form and maintain connections that provide safety and support. In romantic relationships, the release of oxytocin can create a strong sense of attachment, making us feel more secure and connected to our partner. Similarly, in friendships and family relationships, oxytocin helps strengthen bonds and reinforces the brain's message that connection equals safety.

The brain's survival instincts are not solely about keeping us physically safe. They are equally concerned with emotional security. We all have a deep, innate need to feel understood, valued, and accepted by others. When these emotional needs are met, the brain registers the relationship as a source of comfort and protection. However, when these needs go unmet—through rejection, criticism, or neglect—the brain perceives the relationship as a threat to our emotional well-being. This is why the end of a relationship, whether through breakup, conflict, or loss, can feel so devastating. The brain is not only grieving the person, but also the loss of connection, security, and emotional safety.

Interestingly, the brain's survival focus can sometimes lead to self-sabotage in relationships. For instance, if someone has experienced betrayal or abandonment in the past, their brain may become hyper-vigilant to any signs of potential rejection in future relationships. This heightened sensitivity can cause them to misinterpret innocent words or actions as threats, prompting defensive reactions or emotional withdrawal. In this way, the brain's protective instincts—though well-intentioned—can create barriers to building healthy, lasting connections.

Understanding the brain's focus on safety, connection, and bonding can help us navigate relationships with greater awareness. By recognizing that our brain is wired to protect us—sometimes excessively—we can pause and reflect when we feel triggered or defensive. Rather than reacting impulsively, we can remind ourselves that the brain's first priority is survival, and that not every perceived threat is truly dangerous. Moreover, when these feelings or impulses arise, it's important to lean into vulnerability within safe relationships. By sharing our emotions openly, we give ourselves the opportunity to process and release them, rather than act on patterns that no longer serve us.

Ultimately, the brain's survival instincts shape our relationships in profound ways. They drive us to seek connection, form emotional bonds, and secure a sense of safety. But they can also lead us to guard ourselves from perceived dangers, sometimes at the cost of deeper intimacy. By becoming aware of these internal mechanisms, we can learn to balance the brain's need for safety with the heart's desire for connection, paving the way for healthier, more fulfilling relationships.

Attachment Styles: How Our Brains Develop Attachment Styles Based on Early Experiences

The connections we form in our earliest years lay the foundation for how we relate to others throughout life. These early relationships—particularly those with our primary caregivers—play a crucial role in shaping the brain's development of attachment styles, or the patterns that influence how we connect, trust, and bond with others as we grow. Attachment styles are formed through a combination of biology, brain development, and the experiences we have in our formative years. Understanding how these styles emerge can provide valuable insights into our adult relationships and help us navigate them more effectively.

The concept of attachment styles stems from the work of psychologist John Bowlby, who pioneered attachment theory in the mid-twentieth century. His research proposed that human beings have an innate need to form emotional bonds, and that the quality of those early bonds significantly impacts our psychological development. When infants feel secure and have their needs consistently met, they develop a sense of safety in the world, which carries into their relationships later in life. Conversely, inconsistent, neglectful, or chaotic caregiving can lead to insecure attachment patterns, which may affect the ability to form trusting and stable relationships.

From the moment we are born, our brain is programmed to seek connection and security from caregivers. During infancy and early childhood, we are entirely dependent on others to meet our basic needs—food, warmth, comfort, and emotional support. The way caregivers respond to these needs has a lasting impact on brain development and on the patterns we form in social and emotional bonding.

The brain of an infant is highly malleable, rapidly forming neural connections in response to experience. When a caregiver consistently responds to an infant's cries, offers comfort, and meets their needs, the infant's brain learns that the world is a safe and predictable place. This fosters what is known as a secure attachment style, in which the child feels confident exploring their environment, knowing they can rely on their caregiver for support.

However, when a caregiver is inconsistent—sometimes responsive and other times not—the child may develop an insecure attachment style. Unsure whether their needs will be met, the child develops anxious, avoidant, or ambivalent attachment behaviors. (We will explore the details of each style later.) Because the brain constantly seeks patterns and understanding of its environment, it forms an internal model of relationships based on these early interactions. Over time, these attachment patterns become ingrained, shaping how we approach connection, intimacy, and trust in adulthood.

A securely attached child grows up with a strong sense of self-worth and the ability to form healthy, balanced relationships. When a child's brain develops in an environment of consistent nurturing and safety, they learn that others can be trusted and that they are deserving of love and support. This foundation contributes to stability and confidence in future relationships—whether romantic, familial, or social.

In adulthood, individuals with a secure attachment style are generally comfortable with intimacy and vulnerability. They approach relationships with a sense of balance, maintaining a healthy level of independence while still valuing emotional closeness. Because their brain has learned that others are reliable and that conflict can be resolved, they tend to handle relationship challenges with openness, trust, and clear communication.

Secure attachment also fosters emotional resilience. Those with secure attachment are more likely to cope with stress and relational setbacks without falling into patterns of avoidance or overwhelming anxiety. This is because their brain has built a strong association between connection and safety, enabling them to regulate emotions in a way that supports both their needs and the needs of their partners.

In contrast, individuals who experienced inconsistent or neglectful caregiving in early childhood often develop an insecure attachment style. This can manifest in several forms, each of which influences how they relate to others in adulthood:

Anxious-Preoccupied Attachment

Individuals with the anxious-preoccupied attachment style often struggle with feelings of insecurity and a fear of abandonment. As children, they may have experienced caregivers who were inconsistent—sometimes attentive, other times distant or unavailable. This unpredictability wires the brain to expect instability in relationships, leading to heightened anxiety and a persistent need for reassurance. In adulthood, this attachment style may appear as clinginess, over-dependence, and fear that their partner will leave them.

Avoidant Attachment

In contrast, those with an avoidant attachment style often develop a pattern of emotional distance. This typically stems from childhood experiences with emotionally unavailable or dismissive caregivers. The brain adapts by suppressing the need for connection and emphasizing self-sufficiency. As adults, individuals with avoidant attachment may struggle with intimacy, finding it difficult to trust others or open up emotionally. They often keep people at arm's length to protect themselves from potential rejection or disappointment.

Disorganized Attachment

Disorganized attachment is often linked to traumatic or chaotic early experiences. In such cases, the caregiver may be both a source of comfort and fear, creating confusion for the developing brain. This results in an internal conflict where the child simultaneously craves and fears connection. As adults, individuals with disorganized attachment may display unpredictable or erratic behavior in relationships, oscillating between clinginess and emotional withdrawal. They may also struggle with feelings of worthlessness or fear of being hurt.

How Attachment Styles Affect Adult Relationships

Our attachment styles, shaped by early experiences, continue to influence how we approach relationships throughout our lives. They guide how we perceive others, how much we trust them, and how we respond to emotional closeness or distance. The brain, acting as a record of these early interactions, relies on established patterns to navigate new relationships. This is why, even when we consciously desire a different outcome, we may find ourselves repeating familiar behaviors.

For example, someone with an anxious-preoccupied attachment style may struggle with jealousy or possessiveness, fearing that their partner will leave—even in the absence of any evidence. The brain, conditioned by early experiences, associates closeness with the threat of abandonment, triggering anxiety and reactive behaviors.

In contrast, individuals with avoidant attachment may withdraw from partners or resist emotional intimacy, even in healthy, loving relationships. In this case, the brain has learned to associate closeness with vulnerability and potential pain, prompting avoidance as a protective mechanism.

While attachment styles are deeply rooted, they are not unchangeable. Thanks to the brain's ability to form new neural connections (neuroplasticity), we can reshape these patterns through awareness, intentional effort, and new relational experiences. Therapy, supportive relationships, and consistent self-reflection can help individuals shift from insecure attachment patterns toward a more secure style. Over time, this creates new mental pathways that support trust, emotional intimacy, and resilience.

Understanding our attachment style is a powerful first step toward creating healthier relationships. By recognizing how our brain's early wiring influences our present behaviors, we can begin making conscious choices that lead to more fulfilling and secure connections.

This understanding of attachment naturally leads us to a deeper question: how does the brain filter our reality in the first place? This is where the Reticular Activating System (RAS) comes into play. The RAS is a key neurological function that helps us make sense of the world by filtering our experiences through the lens of our beliefs and focus.

The Reticular Activating System (RAS): The Brain's Belief-Based Filter

The Reticular Activating System (RAS) is one of the most fascinating and powerful systems in the human brain. It influences how we perceive reality by filtering the overwhelming amount of sensory information we receive at any given moment. It determines what we consciously notice and what fades into the background.

Though most people may not be familiar with the RAS by name, they experience its effects constantly. It's the reason you can suddenly hear your name in a crowded room or notice a specific car model everywhere after you've decided to buy one. The RAS guides your attention toward information that aligns with your existing beliefs and priorities, whether you're consciously aware of those beliefs or not.

In the context of relationships and personal growth, understanding the RAS is transformative. It helps explain why we tend to find evidence that supports what we already believe, and why those beliefs can become self-fulfilling prophecies. The RAS filters the world through the lens of our internal narrative. If we do not actively challenge and reshape that narrative, the brain will continue to filter in ways that reinforce our current mindset, even when that mindset may be limiting or distorted.

What Is the Reticular Activating System?

The Reticular Activating System (RAS) is a network of neurons located in the brainstem, stretching from the spinal cord up to the thalamus. While its primary role is to regulate wakefulness and sleep–wake transitions, it also functions as a sensory filter, determining what information reaches the conscious mind and what is discarded as background noise. Because we are constantly bombarded with more stimuli than our brains can consciously process, the RAS plays a crucial role in helping us focus on what matters most.

Imagine walking down a busy street. Your senses are overwhelmed by a cacophony of sounds—honking cars, people talking, birds chirping—as well as a flood of visual input from signs, colors, and movement. Yet, despite all this chaos, your brain can zero in on something specific, like a friend waving at you from across the street. That's the RAS in action, filtering out distractions and homing in on what's relevant to you in that moment.

Importantly, the RAS doesn't filter information randomly. It does so based on what the brain deems important. And what the brain deems important is often shaped by our beliefs, values, and lived experiences. These internal frameworks act like a radio dial, tuning our awareness to specific "frequencies" of information while ignoring everything else.

For example, if you believe that the world is a dangerous place, your RAS will heighten your sensitivity to potential threats. You may find yourself drawn to alarming headlines, focused on the negative aspects of your relationships, or hyper-aware of situations that seem risky or uncertain. On the other hand, if you believe the world is full of opportunities, your RAS will filter for those. You'll notice chances for growth, connect more easily with people who share your optimistic outlook, and remain more open to new experiences.

This filtering process begins in early childhood and becomes reinforced over time through repeated experiences. If, as a child, you were frequently told that you are smart and capable, your RAS will continue to seek out information that supports this belief. You'll be more likely to notice opportunities for success, affirmation, and achievement. Conversely, if you were made to feel inadequate or unworthy, your RAS may filter for experiences that reinforce those limiting beliefs, causing you to overlook possibilities or question your capabilities.

The Impact of Beliefs on the RAS

At the core of the RAS's filtering process are our beliefs, those deeply held ideas about ourselves and the world around us. The RAS, in essence, works to confirm these beliefs by selectively focusing on information that supports them. This is why people with different belief systems can experience the same event in completely different ways. Each person's RAS seeks out information that validates their perspective, causing them to perceive entirely different aspects of the same situation.

Consider a relationship in which one partner believes their significant other is supportive and loving, while the other harbors insecurities and doubts about the relationship. The partner with the positive belief is more likely to notice small acts of kindness, gestures of affection, and words of affirmation. In contrast, the insecure partner may focus on moments of distance, perceived slights, or misunderstandings. Though both individuals are experiencing the same relationship, their differing beliefs cause them to filter it through their RAS in vastly different ways, shaping not just what they see, but how they react.

This filtering process becomes even more profound when we consider how the RAS influences not only our perceptions but also our actions. When we expect positive outcomes, we are more likely to take proactive steps toward achieving them, and our brain continues to filter for experiences that reinforce those expectations. On the flip side, if we anticipate failure or disappointment, the RAS will emphasize environmental cues that align with those negative beliefs, often leading to self-sabotage or withdrawal.

One of the most significant effects of the RAS is its role in creating self-fulfilling prophecies. Because the RAS filters information based on our beliefs, we often end up manifesting the very outcomes we expect. If you believe you are destined for success, your RAS will highlight opportunities that support that belief, and you'll be more likely to act on them. Over time, this creates a reinforcing cycle, as your brain continues to seek out and emphasize information that validates your belief in your own success.

The same is true for negative beliefs. If you believe that you are unworthy of love or incapable of achieving your goals, your RAS will filter for evidence that confirms those beliefs. You might unconsciously push away people who try to get close to you, avoid taking meaningful risks, or downplay your achievements—all of which reinforce the original belief. In this way, the RAS plays a central role in creating the reality we experience, whether that reality is empowering or limiting.

The encouraging news is that the RAS is not fixed. It can be trained to focus on new beliefs and possibilities. By consciously choosing to shift your attention, you can reprogram the RAS to filter for more positive and empowering experiences. This process requires both awareness and intentional effort, but over time, the brain can be rewired to prioritize healthier, more constructive patterns of thought.

One powerful way to train the RAS is through affirmations and visualization exercises. By regularly focusing on positive beliefs and desired outcomes, you condition your RAS to scan for experiences that support those beliefs. For example, if you want to develop a stronger sense of worthiness and connection, you might repeat affirmations like "I am deserving of love and meaningful relationships" each day. Gradually, your RAS will begin to spotlight situations and interactions that validate this new belief, helping you engage more confidently and openly with others.

Another effective method is meditation, particularly mindfulness or guided visualization. Meditation helps clear mental clutter and quiet the noise of automatic negative thoughts. When you meditate, you create space to intentionally observe your beliefs and redirect your focus. For example, during a session, you might visualize yourself feeling calm and capable, or imagine welcoming healthy relationships into your life. This practice trains your RAS to filter out distractions and fear-based signals, making it easier to recognize opportunities that align with your goals and inner values.

In relationships, this means being intentional about where we place our attention, rather than fixating on misunderstandings or moments of tension. In this way, we can train our RAS to notice acts of love, gestures of kindness, and opportunities for growth. This shift in perspective not only transforms how we interpret the relationship but also influences how we show up in it, helping to create a more positive and supportive dynamic.

By understanding the role of the RAS in shaping our reality, we gain the ability to take control of our beliefs and, ultimately, our experiences. Instead of passively accepting the default mental filters our brain has developed over time, we can actively choose to reframe our thinking. In doing so, we open ourselves to a world rich with new opportunities, deeper connections, and the potential for profound personal growth.

Chapter 4: Values and Fears

Values act as the guiding compass of our lives, shaping our behaviors, decisions, and ultimately, the direction we take. These core principles influence how we respond to situations, form relationships, and determine what we perceive as right or wrong. Whether we are conscious of it or not, every action we take is driven by a set of internal values that help us navigate life's complexities. They provide the foundation for our beliefs and goals and serve as an anchor, especially in moments of uncertainty. In many ways, values function like a moral compass, pointing us toward choices and paths that feel most aligned with who we are.

At the heart of this lies the fact that values influence our behaviors across all aspects of life: relationships, work, and self-image. When we reflect on the reasons behind our decisions, we often discover that it's our values at work, those deeply held principles we've carried throughout our lives. For instance, if honesty is one of your core values, you might find yourself compelled to speak up even when it's uncomfortable, or to avoid situations that could compromise your integrity. Likewise, if you value loyalty, your actions toward family, friends, and colleagues will be shaped by a strong commitment to those relationships. Every value creates a ripple effect, influencing how we act, how others perceive us, and the expectations we hold for them.

Values are not just abstract ideals, they are closely tied to our emotional responses. They shape how we feel about certain events and interactions. For example, if you value respect and find yourself in a situation where you're disrespected, you may feel anger or frustration. In contrast, someone whose values emphasize conflict avoidance may experience anxiety or a desire to retreat. These emotional reactions to value-based triggers often dictate how we respond, guiding us toward behaviors that either reaffirm our values or challenge us to reassess them.

In relationships, values are central to compatibility and long-term harmony. When our values align with those of the people around us, interactions tend to be more fluid and harmonious. Conversely, conflicting values can create tension. For example, if one partner values ambition and career advancement while the other prioritizes work–life balance, misunderstandings and friction can arise. It's not that either set of values is inherently wrong, but navigating life with differing guiding principles makes compromise more challenging. Many relationships thrive or falter based on the degree to which individuals' values align or evolve together over time.

This is why consciously examining our values is so important. By becoming more aware of what drives us, we not only make better decisions but also avoid being led by values that don't truly reflect who we are. Often, people adopt societal or inherited values without questioning their relevance. For instance, someone might pursue a high-paying career because they grew up in a household that prioritized financial success, only to realize later that personal fulfillment and creativity matter more to them. In this way, our values are not static. They evolve as we grow and accumulate life experience.

It's also worth noting that values can serve as a compass during times of fear or uncertainty. Our core values can help us stay grounded when life presents us with difficult choices such as moving to a new city, leaving a job, or ending a relationship. Reflecting on what truly matters can provide clarity in the face of indecision. Ask yourself: "Does this choice align with what I truly value?" In moments like these, our values become a beacon, guiding us toward decisions that may be difficult but feel right.

However, while values can steer us in the right direction, they can also become barriers if held too rigidly. Some values, especially those inherited or deeply ingrained, may no longer serve us in our current lives. For example, if you were raised in an environment that prized self-reliance to the point of isolation, you might struggle to seek help or form deep connections, even though collaboration and community could significantly support your personal growth. In such cases, re-examining our values and recognizing where they may need to evolve is essential for meaningful personal development.

Values also play a significant role in the workplace and in how we approach professional challenges. A person who values innovation might thrive in environments where creativity is encouraged and rewarded, but could feel stifled in rigid corporate structures that prioritize tradition over experimentation. Conversely, someone who values structure and predictability may excel in roles that demand meticulous planning and attention to detail, yet feel overwhelmed in dynamic, fast-paced settings. Understanding how our values intersect with our work can help guide us toward career paths that align not only with our skills but also with our deeper needs and aspirations.

Moreover, our values influence how we handle ethical dilemmas and moral decisions. When faced with difficult choices—such as reporting unethical behavior at work or standing up for someone who is being mistreated—it is often our values that tip the scale. Individuals who prioritize justice may act swiftly, while those who value harmony above all else might hesitate, fearing the repercussions of disrupting the status quo.

In a world filled with competing demands and external pressures, it's easy to lose sight of our values, or to allow them to be overshadowed by societal expectations. Yet taking the time to reflect on what truly matters is crucial. When our behaviors align with our values, we live more authentically, make decisions with greater clarity and confidence, and foster relationships that reflect our true selves. Values are more than abstract ideals. They are the compass that directs our every step, guiding us through life's challenges with integrity and purpose.

As we transition from understanding how our core values guide our behaviors, it's important to recognize that many of these values are not solely of our own making. In fact, a significant portion of our value system is inherited, passed down from parents, family members, or other influential figures in our early lives. These inherited values often form the foundation on which we construct our own understanding of the world. However, as we grow and encounter new experiences, we begin to adopt new values, or challenge the ones we've been given. This blend of inherited and adopted values ultimately shapes who we are, how we see the world, and how we choose to navigate it.

From the moment we are born, we are exposed to the value systems of those around us, primarily our caregivers. Our parents or guardians are typically the first to show us what is important. They model behaviors, beliefs, and attitudes that we often internalize without conscious awareness. For example, if you grew up in a household where hard work was highly valued, you may find that as an adult you possess a strong work ethic and a drive to succeed. Conversely, if you were raised in an environment where compassion and kindness were emphasized, you might place a higher priority on relationships and emotional connection.

These early influences are powerful, as children are highly impressionable. We look to the adults in our lives not only for behavioral cues but also for guidance on how to interpret and engage with the world. Our parents' values often become the initial lens through which we make sense of our surroundings. For instance, a child whose parents value education may grow up believing that academic achievement is the key to success, while a child raised in a family that celebrates adventure and exploration may develop a deep appreciation for independence and curiosity.

Yet it's not just the overt lessons we learn from our parents that shape our values. Many of the values we inherit are absorbed through observation and subtle cues. Children are incredibly perceptive and often pick up on the unspoken values that govern family dynamics. For example, a parent may never explicitly say that they value financial security, but if they are constantly working long hours and expressing anxiety about money, a child may internalize the belief that financial stability is paramount. These inherited values, whether spoken or unspoken, form the backbone of how we initially understand ourselves and the world.

As we grow older, however, we begin to encounter situations and people that challenge or reinforce the values we inherited. This is where our own experiences start to play a critical role. Perhaps you were raised with the belief that success is defined by wealth and status, but as you moved through adulthood, you met individuals who found fulfillment in artistic pursuits, travel, or community service. These new experiences may prompt you to re-evaluate what you truly value. You might begin to adopt new values that reflect your personal journey, rather than simply carrying forward the ones you inherited.

This process of adopting new values or modifying inherited ones is a natural part of personal growth. Life has a way of testing the values we've been given, compelling us to confront situations where those values no longer serve us. For instance, someone raised to believe in absolute self-reliance may find, in adulthood, that they struggle to ask for help, even when it's necessary. Over time, they may come to value collaboration and community just as much as independence. This shift does not negate the values they were raised with; rather, it adds nuance and depth to their understanding of what truly matters.

Our values are also shaped by cultural, societal, and generational influences. Each generation tends to carry forward certain values from the previous one while simultaneously challenging others. For example, many in older generations grew up valuing stability: securing a steady job, purchasing a home, and settling down. In contrast, younger generations, especially in response to economic and social shifts, may place greater emphasis on flexibility, creativity, and work–life balance. These generational shifts illustrate how values evolve over time, both individually and collectively.

Inherited values can sometimes become sources of inner conflict, especially when they clash with values developed through personal experience. Imagine someone raised in a family that emphasizes tradition and conformity, who then grows to value innovation and individualism. This person may find themselves at odds with their family's expectations, leading to feelings of guilt, confusion, or even resentment. Navigating such differences requires a delicate balance, honoring your roots while staying true to the person you are becoming.

It's also important to recognize that not all inherited values are positive. In some cases, we may absorb values that are limiting or even harmful. For example, someone raised in an environment that prioritizes competition over collaboration may struggle to build meaningful relationships, seeing others as threats rather than allies. Similarly, someone who grew up in a household that placed a high value on appearance may develop insecurities, equating self-worth with physical attractiveness. Recognizing and challenging these inherited values can be a vital step in personal growth and emotional healing.

Ultimately, the values we inherit and adopt form the foundation of our belief system, shaping how we perceive the world and interact with it. However, part of becoming an authentic individual is learning to question those values and determine which ones truly resonate with who we are, and who we want to become. It's not about rejecting the values we were raised with, but about integrating them into a more complete understanding of ourselves in today's world. If we're dissatisfied with where we are in life or with what our lives have become, it may be time to examine the values that have been driving our decisions.

The process of examining and evolving our values is ongoing. As we encounter new experiences, meet different people, and face various challenges, our values naturally shift and grow. The key is to remain open to this evolution, to continuously evaluate our values and allow ourselves the flexibility to adapt, while staying grounded in the principles that truly matter to us. In doing so, we create a value system that honors both where we come from and the person we are striving to become.

Beyond understanding how inherited values shape who we are, it's also important to recognize another powerful force that influences our behavior and relationships: fear. Whether we're aware of it or not, fear plays a significant role in how we navigate the world, especially when it comes to the most vulnerable parts of ourselves: our identity, relationships, and sense of security. These fears are universal. We all experience one or more of them, and they often stem from formative experiences in our past. At the core of many of our struggles lie three common fears: abandonment, self-worth, and trust.

These fears profoundly affect our relationships, or our inability to form them, because they shape how we connect, how much vulnerability we allow, and how we interpret others' actions. Often, these fears drive us to behave defensively, or even to self-sabotage, all in an effort to shield ourselves from pain. But when we fail to acknowledge and address these fears, they can become significant barriers to the meaningful, fulfilling connections we long for.

One of the most deeply rooted and universal fears is the fear of abandonment. This fear can often be traced back to our earliest experiences as children, when our survival depended entirely on the presence and care of others. As infants, we are completely vulnerable, and any disruption, real or perceived, in the bond with our caregivers can leave lasting emotional scars. For example, a child who experiences inconsistent caregiving may grow up with a heightened sensitivity to rejection. As adults, this fear of abandonment can manifest in various ways: becoming overly clingy in relationships, avoiding intimacy altogether to protect against potential loss, or even staying in unhealthy relationships out of fear of being alone.

In romantic relationships, the fear of abandonment can lead to behaviors that ultimately undermine the connection we're trying so hard to preserve. A person who fears being left might become overly dependent on their partner, constantly seeking reassurance; or, conversely, they may push their partner away preemptively, believing abandonment is inevitable. This creates a self-fulfilling cycle: the fear of abandonment leads to behaviors that strain the relationship, increasing the likelihood of the very outcome the person is trying to avoid.

Another universal fear is the fear of self-worth. At its core, this fear centers on questioning whether we are truly lovable, valuable, or deserving of good things. It often stems from early experiences of criticism, lack of support, or feeling like we never measured up to the expectations placed upon us by caregivers. When our sense of self-worth is low, we may struggle to believe that others can love us for who we truly are. This fear can lead us to hide parts of ourselves, people-please, or constantly seek acceptance and validation, fearing that if others saw the "real" us, they would reject us.

In relationships, a lack of self-worth can manifest in many ways. Some people settle for less than they deserve, remaining in unhealthy or toxic relationships because they don't believe they're worthy of something better. Others may overcompensate by constantly trying to prove their worth, going above and beyond to meet their partner's needs while neglecting their own. The fear of not being good enough can also result in relentless comparison, where we measure ourselves against others and feel inadequate or jealous. This type of thinking is destructive, as it prevents us from embracing our authentic selves and from seeking happiness in simply being who we are, believing we are enough in our connections with others.

The final deeply ingrained universal fear is the fear of trust, or more precisely, the fear of betrayal. Trust is the cornerstone of any strong relationship, but for many, trusting others feels like a risk, one that could lead to hurt, disappointment, or betrayal. This fear often stems from past experiences where our trust was broken, whether by a parent, close friend, or romantic partner. At times, it may also originate from a lack of self-trust: the fear that we won't make the right choices or that we cannot rely on ourselves to discern who is worthy of our trust. Whether someone has betrayed us in a formative relationship or we struggle to trust our own judgment, it can be incredibly difficult to trust others.

The fear of betrayal can lead to hypervigilance in relationships, where we're constantly on guard, looking for signs that the other person might hurt us. We may become overly suspicious, question our partner's intentions, or doubt their loyalty. In some cases, this fear may lead to controlling behavior as we attempt to manage or predict the other person's actions in an effort to avoid being blindsided. Unfortunately, this often creates tension and mistrust, driving a wedge between partners and, ironically, increasing the likelihood of the very betrayal we feared.

It's important to recognize that these universal fears of abandonment, self-worth, and trust are natural and deeply human. Everyone experiences them to some extent, as they stem from our fundamental need for safety, connection, and belonging. However, when left unexamined or unaddressed, these fears can hold us back from experiencing the intimacy, depth, and fulfillment we long for in our relationships, and they may even lead to the pain we were trying to avoid.

So, how do we begin to overcome these fears? The first step is to acknowledge them. Often, we're unaware of how much our fears influence our behaviors and decisions. By bringing these fears into conscious awareness, we can begin to understand how they have shaped our past and how they may still be affecting our present. Once we are aware of them, we can start to challenge the beliefs that underlie these fears. A helpful approach is to ask ourselves reflective questions such as: "Is this really true?" and "Why do I believe this?" Through self-inquiry and compassionate reflection, we begin to loosen the grip these fears have on our lives.

For example, if you struggle with the fear of abandonment, ask yourself: Is it true that I am alone? And if it feels true, then why does it feel that way? Did you experience a loss or disruption in a key relationship early in life? How has that fear shaped the way you approach relationships now? By understanding the root of the fear, and discerning whether it is rational or irrational, we can begin to separate past experiences from present reality. It's also helpful to remind yourself that while the fear may feel real, it doesn't always reflect the truth of your current relationships.

In addition to self-awareness, cultivating self-compassion is essential. Many of these fears are tied to feelings of inadequacy or unworthiness. By practicing self-compassion, we learn to treat ourselves with kindness and patience rather than harsh judgment. This practice strengthens our sense of self-worth and reduces the need to seek constant validation from others.

Finally, building trust in relationships requires vulnerability. While it may feel safer to guard ourselves, true intimacy comes from being willing to open up, even in the face of fear. This doesn't mean throwing caution to the wind, but rather taking intentional, measured steps toward trusting others and allowing ourselves to be seen for who we truly are.

Overcoming fear is neither simple nor immediate. Fear is often deeply embedded, rooted in past experiences or long-held beliefs reinforced over time. Although fear is universal, the way it manifests in our lives and relationships can vary greatly. The good news is that with conscious effort, self-awareness, and intentional strategies for growth, we can begin to identify and address the fears that hold us back. Doing so not only enhances our emotional well-being but also opens the door to healthier, more authentic, and more fulfilling relationships.

The First Step: Acknowledging the Fear

The first and perhaps most important step in overcoming any fear is recognizing that it exists. Often, our fears operate in the background of our lives, subtly shaping our thoughts, actions, and decisions without our full awareness. We may feel the effects of fear—hesitation, anxiety, or avoidance—but not fully understand its root cause.

Begin by asking yourself: What am I afraid of?

Is it the fear of rejection? The fear of failure? The fear of not being good enough? Once you've identified the specific fear, try to trace it back to its origin. Did it stem from a particular experience, such as a betrayal or a childhood event? Or was it instilled over time by societal pressures, family expectations, or repeated negative reinforcement?

Journaling can be a helpful tool during this process. By writing down your thoughts, feelings, and fears, you create a space for self-reflection and clarity. As you delve into the sources of your fears, patterns may begin to emerge, offering insight into how those fears have influenced your behaviors and choices.

Reframing the Narrative

Once you've identified your fears, the next step is to reframe how you perceive them. Our fears are often accompanied by stories, narratives we've told ourselves for years. For example, if you fear failure, the story might be: *I'm not smart enough, so I'll never succeed.* If you fear abandonment, the story might be: *Everyone I love will eventually leave me.*

These are limiting beliefs. While they may feel true, they're not necessarily based in reality. A powerful way to combat fear is to challenge these narratives and replace them with more truthful, empowering statements.

Instead of saying, "I'm not good enough," try: "I'm capable, and I'm growing every day."

Instead of believing, *Everyone leaves me*, remind yourself: *I am worthy of love and connection, and I'm learning to trust others.*

This process of reframing helps break the cycle of fear and cultivates a more compassionate, positive outlook. It's important to be gentle with yourself: challenging deep-rooted beliefs can feel uncomfortable, but self-compassion makes transformation possible.

Facing Fear Gradually: Exposure Therapy

One of the most effective methods for overcoming fear is gradual exposure. This involves facing your fear in small, manageable steps rather than avoiding it altogether. For instance, if you fear public speaking, you don't need to jump into giving a speech in front of a large audience. Instead, you might begin by speaking up in small group settings or practicing in front of a trusted friend or family member.

Gradual exposure helps desensitize you to the fear and allows you to build confidence over time. Each small success helps rewire your brain, teaching it that the feared situation is not as dangerous or overwhelming as you once believed.

In relationships, exposure might mean slowly opening up emotionally to build trust. If you've been hurt in the past, it's natural to want to protect yourself. However, avoiding intimacy or vulnerability only reinforces the fear. You create opportunities for connection and healing by gradually allowing yourself to be vulnerable, whether that means sharing your feelings, setting boundaries, or letting others support you.

Fear thrives in uncertainty, and our minds are often quick to jump to the worst-case scenario. Cultivating mindfulness is a powerful strategy for overcoming fear because it encourages us to stay grounded in the present moment, rather than being consumed by anxiety about the future or regret about the past.

Mindfulness involves observing your thoughts and emotions without judgment. When fear arises, instead of suppressing it or reacting impulsively, practice acknowledging it with curiosity. Ask yourself: What is this fear trying to tell me? Is it true that this or that will happen? or What's the worst that can happen? By being present with your fear, you allow yourself to process it more effectively rather than letting it dictate your actions.

In addition to mindfulness, practicing self-awareness in relationships can help you recognize when fear is influencing your behavior. For example, if you notice yourself avoiding a difficult conversation with your partner, ask yourself why. Is it because you're afraid of conflict or rejection? Being honest with yourself enables you to approach the situation with clarity and intention, rather than reacting out of fear.

Another crucial aspect of overcoming fear is seeking support from others. We don't have to face our fears alone. Whether through friends, family, or a therapist, having a strong support system can make all the difference in navigating fear.

In relationships, mutual support fosters a sense of safety and connection. When both partners are open about their fears and insecurities, it creates a foundation of trust and understanding. This transparency allows for more honest communication and paves the way for healing past wounds.

Therapy can also be an invaluable tool for working through deep-rooted fears. A trained therapist provides a safe, non-judgmental space to explore your fears and offers guidance and techniques for reframing and overcoming limiting beliefs.

Visualization is another effective technique for managing fear. By imagining yourself successfully facing a feared situation, you train your mind to expect positive outcomes. For example, if you fear failure, visualize yourself succeeding and feeling confident in your abilities. This creates a mental blueprint for success, making it easier to take action when the time comes.

Similarly, affirmations—positive statements that reinforce self-belief—can help shift your mindset from fear to empowerment. Repeating affirmations such as "I am capable of overcoming challenges" or "I am worthy of love and trust" can gradually rewire your brain to focus on your strengths rather than your fears.

Overcoming fear isn't about eliminating it completely. It's about developing the courage to face it head-on. Fear is a natural part of the human experience, but it doesn't have to control us. By identifying our fears, reframing limiting beliefs, seeking support, and practicing mindfulness, we can begin to break free from the patterns that hold us back.

In relationships, overcoming fear empowers us to show up as our authentic selves, fostering deeper connection and a greater sense of fulfillment. When we acknowledge and address our fears, we reclaim the power to shape our lives and relationships in ways that align with our values, desires, and true potential. It's a journey, but one that leads to greater freedom, resilience, and love.

PART TWO: UNDERSTAND OTHERS

Communication is the heartbeat of all relationships, whether with family, friends, partners, or colleagues. It's a powerful tool that forms the foundation of understanding, trust, and connection. However, if misused or neglected, it can just as easily lead to distance, confusion, and even resentment. That's why it is essential to understand how to use this tool effectively.

The art of communication goes far beyond knowing the right words to say; it's about creating a genuine connection with another person. Mastering this art requires skills that must be practiced and nurtured over time. Effective communication requires active listening, empathy, clarity, honesty, respect, and confidence. They help create meaningful interactions that strengthen relationships and enrich our lives.

Perhaps the most essential element of communication is active listening. Many people believe that communication is simply about talking—delivering a message clearly and expressing one's feelings openly. While that's partly true, deep connection doesn't stem from how well we speak, but rather from how well we listen. Active listening is the art of being fully present, of making the other person feel truly heard. It means focusing not just on the words being said, but also on the emotions and intentions behind them, without prematurely formulating a response.

Active listening allows us to reflect empathy and validate the needs, feelings, and experiences of the other person. It signals that we're setting aside our own agenda. The practice involves avoiding interruptions and resisting the urge to offer immediate solutions or impose our opinions. Instead, we let the speaker express themselves fully before responding, remaining open to different perspectives and interpretations. The better we listen, the more trust we build. It shows others that we genuinely value and respect their point of view. When someone feels heard, it fosters a sense of safety and comfort, encouraging them to open up and share more deeply. This simple act of listening can be transformative in any relationship, allowing people to feel understood on a deeper level.

Think about a time when you felt truly heard: when someone put aside their phone, made eye contact, and gave you their full attention. That experience likely made you feel valued and respected, leaving a lasting sense of connection. When we offer that same level of attentiveness in our relationships, we demonstrate that the other person's thoughts and feelings matter.

While listening is the first step, empathy is what deepens the connection. If you listen without empathy, you make your interlocutor feel like they're shouting into an empty well. So, how do we become genuinely empathetic? Empathy is the ability to step into another person's shoes: to understand and feel what they are experiencing. It means moving beyond our own perspective to view the world through theirs.

In relationships, empathy acts as a bridge between two minds, helping each person feel less alone and more connected. When we express empathy, we validate the other person's experience, letting them know their emotions are real and worthy of acknowledgment.

Compassion takes empathy a step further. While empathy is about understanding someone's pain, compassion involves a desire to ease it. It's the drive to help lighten someone else's burden. Together, empathy and compassion form one of the strongest foundations for building trust. When we respond with compassion to another's hardship, they are more likely to open up to us in the future. In this way, compassion helps dissolve the walls that separate us, reminding us of our shared humanity.

Imagine a friend sharing a challenge they are going through, perhaps a personal failure or a recent loss. The most helpful response may not be to offer solutions or dismiss their feelings with a quick "It will be okay." Instead, a compassionate response might sound like: "That sounds really hard. I can see why you'd feel that way. I'm here for you." This simple validation can be far more comforting than any advice, as it lets the person know they're not alone in their struggle.

Transparency and honesty are equally important in effective communication. Clarity ensures that our message is easily understood, while honesty helps build trust.

By choosing our words carefully and ensuring our intentions are clear, we can prevent unnecessary conflict and confusion. This means not only thinking about what we want to say, but also considering how the other person might interpret our words. Clarity can be as simple as taking a moment to gather our thoughts before speaking or asking whether we're being understood. When others sense that we're making an effort to communicate clearly, they're more likely to trust that we care about the interaction.

When we speak clearly and truthfully, we reduce the chance of misunderstandings. Honesty, however, is an area where many people struggle. There's a common misconception that honesty must always be blunt or unfiltered, giving rise to the expression "brutal honesty." But honesty doesn't have to be harsh. In fact, honesty delivered with kindness is often the most effective. This is what we can refer to as "honesty with compassion."

When we speak honestly, we reveal our authentic selves, allowing others to connect with us on a deeper level. In relationships, honesty without compassion can come across as judgmental, while honesty tempered with empathy can strengthen bonds and foster openness.

Respect and confidence are also essential traits that support positive communication. Respect involves valuing the other person's views, feelings, and autonomy. When we respect someone, we acknowledge that they have a right to their own perspectives and experiences, even when they differ from our own. Respectful communication is grounded in the understanding that each person's voice matters. It helps maintain a sense of equality and balance in relationships.

Respect and confidence often go hand in hand. When we communicate with respect, we create an environment where both parties feel safe to express themselves. In such an environment, confidence can flourish, as each person knows their thoughts and opinions are valued. For example, in a workplace setting, a respectful conversation between team members allows everyone to share their ideas without fear of being shut down or dismissed. In romantic relationships, respecting each other's opinions, even during disagreements, can prevent arguments from escalating and lead to constructive resolutions.

Ultimately, communication is about more than exchanging words; it's about creating a space where connection can thrive. The art of communication is a lifelong journey, but every step we take toward embodying these qualities brings us closer to the people in our lives and strengthens the bonds we share.

However, understanding positive communication isn't possible without also recognizing what constitutes negative communication. While traits like active listening, empathy, and honesty foster strong, healthy relationships, negative communication patterns can just as easily undermine them. These patterns subtly erode trust, create confusion, and can lead to long-term misunderstandings that are difficult to untangle. Recognizing these patterns, understanding their impact, and learning how to avoid them is just as essential to building healthy relationships as practicing positive communication.

Some common negative communication habits to avoid include sarcasm, vagueness, and exaggeration. While often dismissed as harmless, these behaviors can lead to mistrust and conflict, leaving lasting damage in a relationship.

Sarcasm typically involves saying one thing but meaning another, often in a mocking or ironic tone. To some, sarcasm may seem like a lighthearted way to express humor or to avoid addressing a topic directly. However, in relationships, sarcasm often acts as anger disguised as humor, which can lead to misunderstanding and resentment. Because sarcasm requires the listener to interpret not just the words but also the underlying intent, it can easily cause confusion, especially if the listener is already feeling vulnerable or uncertain.

For example, imagine a couple where one partner asks, "Do you think we'll ever save enough for a vacation?" and the other responds, "Oh, sure, right after we buy that mansion." While the words may be intended as a joke, they can easily convey a hidden message: dismissive, skeptical, or even resentful. The partner who initiated the conversation might feel disheartened, as though their hopes and plans were brushed aside or belittled. Repeated exposure to this type of sarcasm can make someone feel unsupported or misunderstood.

In friendships or work settings, sarcasm often creates an invisible barrier. Friends or colleagues may begin to feel they can't take statements at face value. Even in professional environments, where clear communication is essential, sarcasm can muddy understanding, leading coworkers to question each other's intentions and reliability. When communication is clouded by sarcasm, it becomes difficult to build trust and foster collaboration.

Vagueness can be equally damaging. People often use vague language to avoid confrontation, sidestep responsibility, or simply due to discomfort with directness. Phrases like "We'll see," "Maybe," or "I'll get to it later" might seem harmless on the surface, but they can leave others uncertain about expectations or where they stand.

Vague language suggests a reluctance to fully engage or commit to the topic at hand, yet without the boundaries to express that honestly. (We'll explore boundaries more deeply later.) For now, understand that vagueness reflects a lack of engagement. It may show up as unclear responses, avoidance, or even changing the topic instead of addressing it directly.

Imagine being in a relationship where you're consistently told, "I'll think about it," or "Let's deal with it another time," with no follow-up or resolution. Over time, the person on the receiving end may begin to feel sidelined or unimportant, as if their concerns are not worth addressing.

In both romantic and platonic relationships, when you are vague, people don't know what to expect from you, and eventually, they may lose trust in you.

In the workplace, vagueness can lead to missed deadlines, unclear responsibilities, and a lack of accountability. If a supervisor frequently responds with "Just handle it" or "You'll figure it out," employees may feel unsupported, overwhelmed, and unsure of their direction.

Both sarcasm and vagueness are forms of indirect communication that reflect an unwillingness, or inability, to communicate openly and honestly. People sometimes rely on these habits as defense mechanisms, particularly when they feel uncomfortable with vulnerability or conflict. However, learning to recognize when we're being sarcastic or vague gives us the opportunity to pause, reflect, and choose more direct, thoughtful communication.

Exaggeration is another negative communication habit that, while sometimes rooted in good intentions, can ultimately cause more harm than good. When people exaggerate, they stretch the truth, often to make a point or provoke a stronger reaction. This may include embellishing details in a story, overstating problems, or using absolutes like "always" or "never" during conflicts. Although such statements might seem harmless, exaggeration can gradually erode trust by making it difficult for others to discern what is real and what is inflated.

In relationships, exaggeration can make conflicts appear larger than they truly are, creating unnecessary tension. Imagine a couple discussing household chores, and one partner says, "You never help around the house! I'm always doing everything myself." While this may feel true in a moment of frustration, it is likely an exaggeration. The use of "never" and "always" paints a black-and-white picture that overlooks the full reality. These absolutes can cause the other partner to feel unfairly accused or attacked, triggering defensiveness instead of cooperation.

In the workplace, exaggeration can have similarly damaging effects. If a colleague frequently says things like, "This project is a disaster!" or "We're completely falling apart," it can create an atmosphere of panic and hopelessness. Though such remarks may be intended to convey urgency, they often end up demoralizing team members or presenting a distorted view of the situation.

Moreover, when people exaggerate regularly, their credibility comes into question. Colleagues or partners may begin to doubt the accuracy of what's being said, leading to concerns about the person's judgment and reliability.

Exaggeration can also stem from a desire for validation or attention. Some individuals may amplify details in their stories to keep others engaged or to feel more significant. However, when it becomes clear that the truth is being stretched, listeners may feel manipulated or misled. Relationships built on exaggerated claims are often fragile, lacking the foundation of authenticity and mutual respect. When these embellishments are inevitably exposed, they can lead to feelings of betrayal, leaving others with a sense of having been tricked or deceived.

At its core, the issue with exaggeration is that it distorts reality. Consistent exaggeration reflects a lack of honesty, both with oneself and with others. Rather than facing challenges as they are, exaggeration inflates them, generating unnecessary drama or emotional intensity. Over time, this pattern can hinder problem-solving, as individuals become trapped in cycles of overstatement and emotional reaction.

One effective way to overcome the habit of exaggeration is by practicing intentional communication. Instead of turning to sarcasm, we can strive for honesty, even when it feels vulnerable. Rather than being vague, we can choose clarity and transparency. And instead of exaggerating, we can commit to sharing the truth as it is, understanding that authentic connection is far more valuable than any temporary impression we might create.

With time, letting go of these negative patterns can lead to deeper, more fulfilling relationships. People will begin to sense that they can trust us: that our words carry meaning and that we are genuinely committed to meaningful connection. In this way, we foster environments where our words uplift rather than harm, where misunderstandings are minimized, and where trust and respect can truly flourish.

Constructive Expression Techniques

Constructive expression does not aim to suppress or sugarcoat emotions; rather, it encourages expressing them with clarity and empathy. This approach helps bridge gaps in understanding and avoids unnecessary conflict.

To communicate constructively, we must develop specific skills that foster mutual respect and connection. Three particularly effective techniques include:

1. Using "I feel" statements: Shifting the focus from blame to personal experience helps others understand our emotions without becoming defensive.

2. Maintaining a non-judgmental attitude: This creates a safer space for open dialogue, encouraging empathy and understanding.

3. Identifying the underlying needs behind criticism: Recognizing the unmet needs that drive critical remarks enables us to respond with compassion and work toward real solutions.

By applying these tools, we can shift the tone of our conversations from reactive to receptive, paving the way for stronger, more constructive relationships.

"I Feel" Statements: Communicating Emotions Without Assigning Blame

One of the simplest yet most effective techniques for constructive communication is the use of "I feel" statements. By focusing on our own emotions and experiences rather than assigning blame, these statements promote a more introspective and non-confrontational approach to discussing issues. This, in turn, helps us avoid triggering the defensiveness that blame-based language often provokes.

Consider the difference between saying, "You never listen to me," and "I feel unheard when I'm sharing something important, and it makes me feel disconnected." The first statement places the listener on the defensive, as though they are being accused of wrongdoing. In contrast, the second shifts the focus to the speaker's emotions, allowing the listener to understand the impact of their behavior without feeling attacked. This subtle change opens the door to meaningful dialogue, as both parties feel safer and more respected.

"I feel" statements also promote self-reflection by requiring us to identify and articulate our own emotions. Instead of lashing out, we take a moment to acknowledge what we're feeling, whether it's frustration, sadness, or disappointment. This practice of emotional awareness can help prevent escalation, making it easier to communicate calmly and thoughtfully. By focusing on our own experiences and needs, we invite others into a solution-oriented conversation.

For instance, in a relationship, when one partner says, "I feel overwhelmed when we have so many responsibilities and could use some support," they are expressing a need without making their partner feel inadequate or criticized. This type of communication not only fosters harmony but also encourages mutual problem-solving and empathy.

Non-Judgmental Attitudes: Emphasizing Understanding over Criticism

Approaching communication with a non-judgmental attitude is another essential key to constructive expression. This mindset allows us to listen without forming immediate opinions or assumptions about another person's intentions. When we communicate non-judgmentally, our focus shifts from evaluating to understanding, helping others feel safe to share their genuine thoughts and emotions.

In practice, this can be as simple as resisting the urge to interrupt or respond with skepticism. For example, when a friend shares a personal struggle or experience, our role is to be present, offering support rather than solutions or judgments. A non-judgmental approach recognizes that each individual's experiences and feelings are valid, even if they differ from our own. By showing respect for others' perspectives, we encourage openness and trust.

In relationships, adopting a non-judgmental stance can help us avoid jumping to conclusions based on limited information. Rather than assuming the worst when someone cancels plans or seems distracted, we can approach them with curiosity and care, asking thoughtful questions that show genuine concern. This attitude also enables us to engage in difficult conversations with greater patience and compassion, focusing on understanding rather than reacting.

A practical tool for non-judgmental communication is reflective listening: paraphrasing or repeating back what someone has said to confirm understanding. For example, if a family member says they're feeling overwhelmed, you might respond with, "It sounds like things have been really challenging for you lately. Do you want to talk more about it?" This response communicates empathy without imposing advice or judgment, creating space for honest dialogue and emotional connection.

Behind Criticism Lies a Need: Recognizing and Addressing Underlying Needs in Criticism to Build Connection

Criticism can be one of the most challenging aspects of communication, often leading to defensiveness, hurt feelings, and misunderstandings. However, a closer examination reveals that criticism frequently stems from unmet needs or unexpressed emotions. When we learn to look beyond the surface of critical remarks, we begin to see and understand the underlying needs that drive them.

Consider a scenario in which a partner says, "You're always on your phone, and you never pay attention to me." While the statement may come across as harsh or accusatory, it likely points to a deeper need for connection and presence. Instead of reacting defensively, the listener might respond with empathy: "It sounds like you're feeling disconnected and need more of my attention." This response shifts the focus from blame to understanding, allowing both partners to address the root issue rather than getting caught in conflict.

Addressing the needs behind criticism requires us to approach conversations with empathy and a willingness to look beyond the words being spoken. Often, criticism signals that the other person feels neglected, undervalued, or insecure. By recognizing these needs, we can respond in ways that build trust instead of escalating tension. Rather than dismissing criticism as unfair or unwarranted, we can ask questions that invite deeper dialogue, such as, "Can you tell me more about what's bothering you?" or "What can I do to help you feel more supported?"

In professional settings, understanding the needs behind criticism can improve team dynamics and create a more collaborative environment. For example, if a colleague says, "This isn't going to work," the underlying concerns may relate to feasibility, available resources, or lack of clarity. Instead of dismissing the feedback, a response like, "Can you share your concerns? I'd like to understand better," can foster trust and mutual respect.

Recognizing the needs behind criticism also helps us be more compassionate with ourselves. When we find ourselves feeling critical, examining our own unmet needs can lead to greater self-awareness and healthier communication. For instance, if we feel resentful toward a friend for not reaching out, we might realize we're seeking reassurance and connection. Instead of expressing frustration, we could say, "I've been feeling disconnected lately and would love to catch up."

Constructive communication doesn't mean suppressing emotions or avoiding conflict—it means expressing ourselves with honesty, respect, and empathy. By using "I feel" statements, maintaining a non-judgmental attitude, and exploring the needs behind criticism, we create space for deeper understanding and connection. These practices are simple in theory but require ongoing effort, patience, and a willingness to be vulnerable.

As we integrate these approaches into our daily interactions, we not only improve our communication skills but also deepen our relationships. Constructive expression becomes a foundation for connections where people feel seen, valued, and understood. In doing so, we move beyond surface-level exchanges and build bonds that are resilient, supportive, and genuinely meaningful.

Chapter 2: Emotional Mastery in Relationships

Navigating relationships to keep them healthy is one of the most complex aspects of life's journey. In every interaction, we must balance our needs, emotions, and perceptions with those of others. While intellect and interpersonal skills support us in handling relationship dynamics, emotional intelligence plays an equally vital role. Emotional intelligence—or mastery over our emotions—is the ability to understand, manage, and connect with emotions effectively.

Emotional intelligence in relationships helps us respond thoughtfully and avoid unnecessary conflict. A key element of emotional intelligence is mindfulness: the ability to remain grounded in the present moment and manage our responses with intentionality.

Mindfulness in relationships is not simply about being physically present; it involves deep engagement, attentiveness, and openness, both to ourselves and to the other person. It empowers us to listen deeply, respond calmly, and create a space where emotions can be shared safely. Two crucial aspects of mindfulness in connection are presence and non-reactivity, each playing a significant role in cultivating healthier, more balanced relationships.

When we talk about "being present" in relationships, we often equate it with paying attention. But true presence goes beyond physical proximity or casual listening. It means immersing ourselves fully in the moment, acknowledging our thoughts and emotions without allowing them to control our behavior. Presence involves engaging with the other person as a whole, empathetic being, not simply reacting to stimuli.

Consider a situation where one partner brings up a difficult topic. Rather than becoming defensive or rushing to respond, mindful presence calls for a pause, to breathe and genuinely listen. It means setting aside distractions, whether it's our phones, our mental to-do lists, or the inner dialogue about what we want to say next. Presence is about creating a mental space where we can attune not only to the words being spoken but also to the emotions and intentions behind them.

Staying present also involves openness to our own emotional experience. True engagement can heighten our awareness of discomfort, vulnerability, or defensiveness. Instead of brushing these feelings aside, presence invites us to acknowledge them without judgment. We might think, "I'm feeling defensive right now," or "This is bringing up insecurity." By naming and acknowledging these emotions in real time, we prevent them from bubbling into reactive responses that may harm the relationship. This kind of self-awareness is a cornerstone of calm and thoughtful communication.

Presence takes practice. Our minds are easily distracted, and emotions often pull us in different directions. Developing presence as a habit means consistently choosing to focus on the moment, even during conflict. This commitment to full engagement communicates respect and care. It sends the message: You matter. You are worthy of my attention.

Non-reactivity is another cornerstone of emotional intelligence, particularly in relationships where emotions often run high. At its core, non-reactivity is about resisting the impulse to respond immediately, especially in emotionally charged situations. Instead of reacting based on our first instinct or letting emotions dictate our words, we take a moment to pause, reflect, and choose a response that aligns with our values and goals for the relationship.

Non-reactivity might sound simple in theory, but in practice, it requires conscious effort, particularly in close relationships. In these connections, we may feel deeply invested, vulnerable, or easily triggered, which makes it more challenging to stay calm and objective. However, by making a habit of pausing before responding, we build resilience against reacting impulsively. This pause allows us to examine our emotions and decide how best to communicate our feelings constructively.

Imagine a scenario where a couple is discussing finances, a topic that can often be sensitive. One partner might express frustration about overspending, perhaps unintentionally causing the other to feel judged or inadequate. The immediate reaction might be defensive: "I don't overspend! You're always nitpicking." But by pausing and choosing non-reactivity, the partner could instead take a breath, acknowledge the initial frustration, and consider a more productive response. They might say, "I understand why this concerns you. Let's talk about ways we can address it together." This approach doesn't ignore the problem—it invites collaboration rather than conflict.

Practicing non-reactivity means becoming more aware of our triggers: those words, actions, or situations that elicit strong emotional responses. When we recognize a trigger, we can consciously choose to respond differently rather than fall into familiar patterns of defensiveness or aggression. Over time, this practice builds emotional resilience, allowing us to handle difficult conversations without feeling overwhelmed or losing control.

Non-reactivity is particularly valuable in family relationships, where long-standing patterns and unhealed wounds may become triggers. When a family member makes a critical or hurtful comment, our instinct may be to lash out or shut down. However, by pausing before responding, we might realize that the comment wasn't intended to hurt us—or that the best way to respond is with a calm, non-defensive answer. In some cases, choosing not to respond at all may be the most powerful expression of non-reactivity, showing that we won't allow someone else's behavior to disturb our peace.

When one partner consistently practices non-reactivity, it creates a stable environment where both individuals feel safer discussing challenging topics. This sense of safety is essential for intimacy and emotional closeness. It reassures both people that they can be vulnerable without fear of a reactive response.

Non-reactivity also helps break the cycle of tit-for-tat exchanges that often damage relationships. This doesn't mean suppressing emotions or avoiding important conversations—it means choosing when and how we respond, ensuring that our words are intentional and constructive.

Impermanence: Embracing the Moment in Relationships

"Life goes on" is not just a cliché, it's a truth. Nothing in life stays the same: emotions, circumstances, and even relationships evolve. While this understanding can be unsettling, it also contributes to personal growth and resilience. Accepting change and embracing the mantra "This too shall pass" allows us to face relationship challenges with grace.

Change is one of the few constants in life. Even though we know this, change still often catches us by surprise. We tend to hold on to certain expectations or ideas about our relationships. We assume that our partner, friend, or family member will remain the same, or that our connection will always feel the same. In reality, every relationship is dynamic, shaped by the continuous flow of life's events and personal development. Accepting this truth helps us release some of the fear and anxiety that comes from clinging to a specific outcome.

In relationships, accepting impermanence doesn't mean anticipating the end or emotionally distancing ourselves. Rather, it involves embracing a mindset that welcomes the natural ebb and flow of feelings, situations, and phases. When we acknowledge that everything, including our relationships, will evolve, we become better prepared to meet changes with an open heart. This perspective allows us to appreciate the present moment without trying to grasp or control the future. By letting go of rigid expectations about "how things should be," we open ourselves to deeper, more authentic connections.

Imagine a couple who have been together for years, navigating shifting careers, changing family dynamics, and personal growth. If they rigidly expect each other to remain exactly as they were when they first met, they may experience frustration or disappointment when differences arise. However, if they view these changes as natural, and even positive, aspects of growth, they can support one another through life's transitions. This flexibility not only fosters mutual understanding but also helps prevent monotony in the relationship.

"This Too Shall Pass": A Mindset for Managing Highs and Lows in Relationships

The phrase "This too shall pass" serves as a timeless reminder of impermanence. It applies to both the joys and the struggles of relationships, encouraging a balanced, resilient approach to emotional ups and downs. This mindset helps us savor the highs with gratitude and endure the lows with patience.

In relationships, it's easy to become overly attached to moments of happiness. While there's nothing wrong with cherishing joyful experiences, "This too shall pass" reminds us not to cling so tightly that we lose sight of the present.

Conversely, when relationships face difficulties such as misunderstandings, conflicts, or periods of emotional distance, this mantra reminds us that these struggles are temporary. Rather than feeling trapped or overwhelmed, we can face challenges with a broader perspective, recognizing that they are just one chapter in a longer story. This mindset fosters both patience and resilience.

Take, for example, a disagreement between friends. In the heat of the moment, both may feel hurt or frustrated, and the argument might seem to define the relationship. But by remembering "This too shall pass," they can regain composure, take time to cool down, and return to the conversation later with fresh perspective, understanding that one conflict doesn't define an entire friendship.

Ultimately, the mantra "This too shall pass" is a powerful tool for maintaining emotional stability in relationships. It grounds us amid change and prevents us from being overly influenced by fleeting external circumstances.

Accepting impermanence requires us to engage in daily practices that remind us of life's ever-changing nature. In relationships, this might mean taking the time to appreciate small moments of connection—a heartfelt conversation, a shared laugh, or even quiet companionship. This approach helps us remain present in these experiences without attaching expectations to them. We can remind ourselves, "This moment is valuable just as it is," and find contentment without needing it to last.

On a practical level, embracing impermanence also involves letting go of past grievances or disappointments. In every relationship, conflicts or misunderstandings can leave behind lingering feelings of hurt or resentment. Holding onto these emotions can prevent us from moving forward. When we accept that the past cannot be changed and choose to release these attachments, we make space for new, positive experiences. This doesn't mean ignoring past issues; rather, it means addressing them, learning from them, and ultimately letting them go.

Mindfulness practices such as meditation or journaling can also help us internalize the concept of impermanence. These practices encourage us to observe our thoughts and emotions with detachment, cultivating a greater sense of peace and perspective.

Detachment: Accepting Others and Refining Inner Balance in Relationships

In the realm of relationships, detachment is often misunderstood as emotional distance or indifference. In truth, healthy detachment is about cultivating a balanced relationship between connection and individuality. At its core, it invites us to accept others fully, without trying to change them.

This kind of detachment empowers us to build authentic, meaningful connections while freeing us from the burden of expectations, disappointments, and the need to control outcomes. In many ways, detachment opens the door to true acceptance.

One of the greatest gifts we can offer in any relationship is the acceptance of the other person as they truly are. We often enter relationships with subconscious ideals or expectations, hoping the other person will conform to our vision of who they should be. But every individual is unique, shaped by their own experiences, values, and desires. When we attempt to mold someone into our ideal, we're not engaging with the person in front of us; we're interacting with a version that exists only in our minds.

True acceptance requires us to set aside our personal agendas and embrace others in their full, authentic form.

Of course, this level of acceptance isn't always easy. It challenges us to release the urge to "fix" or "improve" the other person, especially when we disagree with their choices or believe they'd be happier if they changed. For instance, if a partner is introverted and prefers quiet weekends at home, it may be tempting to push them toward a more social lifestyle. However, doing so can diminish their sense of self and breed resentment or inadequacy. Instead, recognizing and honoring their nature—while appreciating the unique strengths it brings to the relationship—can deepen connection and understanding.

Acceptance does not mean tolerating harmful behaviors or neglecting our own needs. Rather, it means allowing others to define and walk their own path.

Healthy detachment also fosters equanimity, a state of inner calm. When we avoid making our peace and happiness entirely dependent on another person's actions, we cultivate a steady mind. This resilience allows us to remain grounded even amid emotional turbulence. Equanimity doesn't mean suppressing our emotions or becoming numb to them. Instead, it involves creating the mental space to observe our feelings without being overwhelmed by them.

This form of detachment offers both individuals a profound sense of freedom. It lifts the mental burden of unmet expectations and unresolved disappointments.

In romantic relationships, for example, detachment may involve releasing the belief that one partner must fulfill all of our emotional needs. We learn to deeply value the connection we share, while also understanding that we are whole and complete on our own. This mindset alleviates the anxiety that can come with emotional dependency.

Detachment is not an overnight transformation, it is a continual practice rooted in self-awareness, patience, and commitment.

Ultimately, the balance between connection and independence enables us to experience the richness of relationships without losing ourselves in them.

Patience and Tolerance

Tolerance is an essential ingredient in any healthy relationship. Building tolerance doesn't mean we have to agree with everything our loved ones say or adopt their perspectives. Instead, it means staying calm and accepting in the face of differences.

One of the greatest tests of tolerance is understanding that people come from varied backgrounds, each carrying unique values, habits, and beliefs. In moments of disagreement, tolerance reminds us that there is often no definitive "right" or "wrong" way to be, just different ways of seeing and responding to the world. When we accept that our loved ones bring their own form of wisdom to the relationship, even if it differs from ours, we foster a connection rooted in mutual respect rather than judgment.

Patience goes hand in hand with tolerance, allowing relationships to develop naturally without feeling forced or rushed. In today's fast-paced world, patience has become a rare quality, yet it remains one of the most vital aspects of sustaining meaningful relationships. When we approach interactions with patience, we create a safe, pressure-free space where growth and connection can unfold organically.

In relationships, patience and tolerance also give us the space to "test the waters": to observe how others behave across various situations. This process helps us understand the deeper layers of a person's personality, beyond initial impressions or surface-level interactions. By taking time to observe without rushing to conclusions, we gain a more realistic, well-rounded understanding of who they are and what we can expect from the relationship.

"Testing the waters" isn't about judging others or expecting them to prove themselves. Rather, it's a gentle and mindful way of appreciating the depth and complexity of another person. For example, watching how someone responds to stress, celebrates achievements, or interacts with different kinds of people can reveal important aspects of their values and priorities. This knowledge equips us to approach the relationship with greater awareness, helping us avoid the common traps of idealization or assumption.

Chapter 3: **Building Compassionate Connections**

Human connection is one of the most precious gifts we can experience. In a world where relationships often feel rushed, shallow, or transactional, the value of deep, compassionate connections is beyond words. Building such connections requires more than surface-level interactions; it calls for courage, compassion, and a willingness to be vulnerable. These elements form the foundation of emotional intimacy, allowing relationships to thrive beyond mere companionship or convenience.

Compassionate connection is the recognition that we all seek a space where we can be our authentic selves, free from fear of judgment. It's a space where empathy replaces criticism, and vulnerability is met with understanding rather than rejection.

This kind of intimacy becomes a powerful buffer against the competitive mindset that can quietly erode relationships.

Connection has the power to lift our spirits, heal our wounds, and give us strength in times of need. But true connection goes far beyond physical presence. It's about emotional presence: opening up, allowing ourselves to be truly seen, and giving others the same opportunity.

Yet this openness requires courage. Sharing our struggles, fears, and dreams means stepping into vulnerability and trusting that our honesty will be met with compassion.

In essence, courage, compassion, and vulnerability are the three pillars of emotional intimacy.

Building compassionate connections begins with the courage to be vulnerable. Vulnerability is often misunderstood as weakness, but in reality, it is one of the bravest acts we can offer. When we reveal our authentic selves without knowing how others will respond, we are expressing trust and a genuine desire to be understood. That is the first step toward emotional intimacy.

Compassion acts as the bridge that helps us accept each other's vulnerability. When we meet others with compassion, we offer comfort instead of criticism, understanding instead of judgment. Compassion says, "I see your struggles, and I'm here with you." It is a quality that gently dissolves barriers and fosters closeness.

For many people, authentic connection is shadowed by the fear of rejection or judgment. We worry that our flaws, insecurities, or past mistakes make us unworthy of love or acceptance. But when we choose to be vulnerable and respond to others with compassion, we create a safe space for mutual understanding and emotional intimacy.

As Brené Brown famously said, "Vulnerability is not winning or losing; it's having the courage to show up when you can't control the outcome." In compassionate relationships, we show up for each other, even when there are no guarantees, and that simple act strengthens the bond.

One of the most liberating aspects of compassionate connection is its ability to reduce rivalry within relationships. Even in close bonds, an unspoken sense of competition can arise: the urge to be right, to be better, or to win. This mindset, while common, creates distance, shifting focus away from shared understanding and support, and toward personal validation.

But in relationships rooted in compassion and emotional connection, the need to compete fades. We no longer feel the urge to prove ourselves, because we know we are valued not for what we achieve or how we compare, but for who we truly are.

Building emotional intimacy takes time and intentional effort. It involves sharing our experiences openly, listening with full presence, and making a conscious choice to understand rather than judge.

And above all, it means choosing compassion, again and again.

Compassion is often viewed as an outward-facing practice: something we offer to others. However, true compassion begins within, with self-compassion. Without a compassionate relationship with ourselves, our efforts to be kind to others can feel forced or insincere. Self-compassion teaches us to extend the same kindness and understanding we give to others to ourselves. It involves recognizing our own struggles, forgiving our mistakes, and embracing a sense of worth that isn't dependent on external validation.

Importantly, self-compassion is not about self-indulgence or excusing harmful behavior. Rather, it's about treating ourselves with the same care we would offer a close friend. It's about acknowledging that, like everyone else, we are imperfect, that we face challenges and deserve support.

The beauty of self-compassion is that it allows us to approach relationships from a place of wholeness rather than need. When we feel secure and cared for, we don't seek others to fill gaps in our sense of self-worth. This not only makes us less reactive but also more patient and understanding. We're able to offer compassion without expecting anything in return, creating a foundation of unconditional support in our relationships.

Self-compassion also empowers us to set healthy boundaries. Many people struggle to say no or to withstand criticism, fearing it will damage relationships or self-image. But when we practice self-compassion, we recognize that protecting our well-being is not selfish, it's essential for sustainable, authentic relationships.

Healthy boundaries are the silent champions of strong relationships. They create a space where individuals feel safe, respected, and understood. Boundaries are not walls that shut people out, but frameworks that define where one person ends and another begins, allowing both partners to coexist with their thoughts, feelings, and identities intact.

A boundary is simply a guideline: an invisible line that communicates what we are and aren't comfortable with. This could mean saying no to certain requests, setting limits on time spent together, or asking for respect around personal values and beliefs.

Boundaries don't restrict love or connection; they protect it. By defining our limits and honoring those of others, we can show up as our authentic selves, without fear of being overshadowed or disrespected.

Establishing boundaries begins with self-awareness. To communicate what feels right or wrong, we must first understand ourselves well enough to recognize our needs. This awareness often comes from reflecting on past experiences, noticing what brings us joy or discomfort, and being honest about our vulnerabilities.

At its core, setting boundaries is an act of self-respect. It's a recognition that we have worth, and that our feelings and well-being matter just as much as anyone else's. This respect for ourselves naturally extends to respecting the boundaries of others.

When we treat boundaries as an expression of self-respect, we can let go of the guilt that sometimes accompanies setting limits. Many people believe that boundaries are selfish or unkind. In reality, they are among the most respectful things we can offer, to both ourselves and others.

Boundaries are most effective when expressed openly and positively. For example, rather than saying, "You can't keep calling me all the time," you might say, "I really value our conversations, but I need some quiet time in the evenings to recharge. Could we talk at a time that works better for both of us?" This approach clarifies your need without creating unnecessary tension or sounding like rejection.

Another vital aspect of boundary communication is consistency. Once a boundary is established, it's essential to follow through. Inconsistent boundaries can lead to confusion, as others may not know what to expect or may feel hurt if limits shift without explanation.

A common myth about boundaries is that they distance people or create barriers to intimacy. In reality, when applied thoughtfully, boundaries can enhance intimacy by allowing people to connect authentically. They help prevent the kind of clinginess that stifles individuality, enabling each person in the relationship to maintain a sense of independence while fostering closeness.

For example, consider a couple who values both alone time and shared time. By establishing boundaries that respect each other's need for personal space, they're more likely to appreciate the moments they spend together. This dynamic encourages both individuals to explore their own interests and passions without feeling guilty or obligated to be constantly available.

Boundaries also protect emotional intimacy by preventing unhealthy patterns such as codependency. When one person's sense of self becomes overly dependent on the relationship, they may begin to sacrifice their own needs to keep the other person happy. Over time, this can lead to resentment, burnout, and a loss of identity. Clear boundaries help avoid this dynamic by ensuring each person takes responsibility for their own happiness and well-being, allowing willingness to take the place of obligation.

At its heart, respecting someone's boundaries is a profound act of kindness and love. It demonstrates that you honor their needs and are willing to adapt your behavior to create a safe, comfortable space for them.

In the end, boundaries are not about creating distance or limiting love. They are about fostering an environment where love and connection can flourish in a healthy, sustainable way.

Chapter 4: Differences and Projections

Our perceptions, beliefs, and attitudes often reflect in our relationships in unexpected ways. This phenomenon is known as projection, a complex but essential concept to understand if we want to build successful relationships.

Projections reveal how our inner world shapes our view of others. We must be mindful of how we sometimes interpret others' actions through the lens of our own beliefs and experiences. By recognizing and managing these tendencies, we can avoid unnecessary conflict and reduce misunderstandings.

Projection occurs when we unconsciously attribute our own feelings, attitudes, or assumptions to someone else. This often happens when we carry unprocessed emotions or unresolved issues. Rather than facing these feelings head-on, our minds seek ways to externalize them, leading us to "see" them in others. While projection is a natural psychological defense mechanism, it can blur reality and distance us from truly understanding those around us.

When we become aware of our projections, we can begin to discern what is genuinely happening in the relationship versus what may simply be a reflection of our inner state.

For example, if we're experiencing self-doubt, we might assume our partner is questioning us, even if they've shown no such signs. Or, if we're feeling insecure about a decision, we might perceive criticism from friends who aren't being critical at all. Recognizing these projections allows us to take a step back and view our relationships more clearly, creating space to build them on healthier ground.

One of the fundamental truths about projection is that we often get what we give. The energy we bring into our interactions can create a feedback loop. If we approach others with trust, kindness, and respect, we're more likely to receive those qualities in return. Conversely, when we project fear, suspicion, or negativity, we may unintentionally create an environment where those emotions flourish on both sides.

Imagine entering a conversation with suspicion. The other person may pick up on your guardedness and respond in kind, only reinforcing your initial suspicion. Our attitudes send signals that others react to, whether consciously or not.

It's empowering to realize that we have the ability to influence the tone of our relationships through our own projections. This doesn't mean that every reaction from others is solely about us, but our attitudes and beliefs can significantly shape how relationships unfold.

In relationships, openness and curiosity are powerful antidotes to projection. Instead of assuming what someone feels or thinks, we can ask questions and seek to understand. When we focus on getting to know each other without preconceived judgments, we build a connection rooted in authenticity rather than distorted by projection.

Your Attitude Reflects You, Not Me

It's essential to remember that people's reactions to us often reveal more about them than they do about us. This realization can be freeing. When we recognize that others' attitudes and responses may stem from their own experiences, beliefs, or unresolved emotions, we're less likely to take things personally. This is not to dismiss our impact on others, but to understand that their behavior may be shaped by factors outside our control.

For instance, if someone reacts negatively to a suggestion, their response might be rooted in past experiences where they felt criticized or unheard. Their reaction isn't necessarily a rejection of our ideas, but rather a reflection of their personal history. By adopting this perspective, we can approach interactions with empathy and curiosity instead of defensiveness. Rather than feeling hurt or frustrated, we can ask ourselves, "Is there something going on for them that I might not be seeing?"

This perspective invites us to engage in relationships with compassion and patience, recognizing that we all carry our own histories and struggles. When we stop taking others' attitudes personally, we free ourselves from unnecessary stress and gain the ability to respond with calmness rather than emotional reactivity. This makes us more supportive partners, friends, and colleagues.

Learning to recognize and own our projections requires a commitment to self-reflection and emotional honesty. It's easy to assume that our interpretations are accurate, especially when strong emotions are involved. However, by pausing and questioning our assumptions, we begin to differentiate what is genuinely happening from what we might be projecting.

One effective way to build this awareness is through mindful reflection. When a reaction feels unusually intense, it's worth asking, "Is there something in my past influencing how I feel right now?" or "Am I responding to this person, or to something unresolved within myself?" By examining our responses, we become better equipped to distinguish between genuine relationship issues and personal projections.

Self-awareness doesn't mean we'll eliminate projections entirely—after all, they are a natural part of the human experience. However, with practice, we can reduce their impact on our relationships, allowing us to approach others with greater clarity and kindness.

Understanding projection also helps us accept differences without judgment. When we recognize that others' behaviors and attitudes are shaped by their unique experiences, we're more inclined to accept them as they are, rather than imposing our expectations on them.

Each person in our lives brings a distinct set of beliefs, values, and experiences. By accepting these differences with an open heart, we create space for relationships that are richer and more diverse. Acceptance doesn't mean we have to agree with everything, but it does mean respecting others' right to their own perspectives.

Recognizing Authority Dynamics

Certain past experiences give rise to the concept of authority in relationships, which can be both strengthening and challenging. Authority, in its healthiest form, establishes trust and clarity, helping us understand boundaries and expectations within our connections. However, authority can also bring tension, especially when it evokes memories of times when control, trust, or power were misused.

For many, authority has represented imbalance, where one person's influence overshadowed another's autonomy. Understanding how authority affects us, and how we respond to it, is essential for building balanced relationships that value mutual respect over control.

Our responses to authority are often shaped by early experiences. For some, authority was a steady presence that offered security, guidance, and a sense of stability. For others, it was a source of tension: parents, teachers, or guardians may have misused their positions to impose strict control, leaving them feeling powerless or unheard. These formative experiences profoundly influence how we perceive and interact with authority in adulthood.

Imagine someone who, as a child, struggled under rigid, unyielding parental rules. As an adult, they may instinctively rebel against authority figures or dominant partners, even if the authority in question is supportive or well-meaning. Authority, to them, feels like something to resist rather than something that can enrich a relationship. This resistance is not necessarily a reflection of the present dynamic but often a projection of past experiences.

Often, we don't recognize these patterns in ourselves, yet they influence our reactions and our willingness to trust.

Conversely, someone who experienced nurturing authority figures may welcome structure in relationships, associating authority with support, wisdom, and guidance. For these individuals, authority is not something to fear but something to appreciate, especially when it's expressed through collaboration and mutual respect.

In any relationship, understanding our personal history with authority can help us identify where our tendencies stem from. Are we inclined to rebel when we feel boundaries or expectations are being set, even if they're intended to benefit us? Do we resist well-meaning guidance from a friend, partner, or mentor because it feels controlling? Recognizing these tendencies gives us a clearer path forward.

In relationships, honesty can sometimes become a way of exerting authority, especially when we feel that our role or experience entitles us to offer "unfiltered" feedback. But the how and when of honesty matter. Sharing truthful thoughts during a heated moment, for example, can result in sharper, more hurtful words than we intend.

Healthy relationships thrive on balance rather than rigid authority. When we view authority as something shared—not imposed—we open ourselves to deeper connection. This approach fosters collaboration over command, and curiosity over assumption.

Reimagining authority in this way invites us to develop a new kind of leadership in relationships, one rooted in respect, empathy, and shared goals. It shifts us away from outdated notions of authority as control and instead presents it as an invitation to trust, mutual growth, and connection.

The Masculine and Feminine Energies in Relationships

With the concept of authority often comes the idea of masculine and feminine energies, even in today's modern era. In every relationship, there exists a dance of energies. These energies are often associated with traits commonly labeled as masculine and feminine, which—despite the names—are not restricted by gender.

Both men and women can embody these qualities. When embraced consciously, these energies complement and balance each other, creating a harmony that strengthens relationships. When partners understand and respect these energies within one another, they open the door to deeper connection and intimacy.

At its core, masculine energy is typically characterized by action, direction, and stability. It seeks purpose, values achievement, and brings a focused clarity that helps navigate life's challenges with confidence. In contrast, feminine energy is receptive and intuitive. It thrives on connection, values emotional expression, and offers empathy that deepens understanding.

In relationships, these energies combine and interplay, helping each partner meet the other's emotional and relational needs. When both partners embrace this balance, they contribute unique strengths that allow each to feel valued, respected, and truly seen.

Honoring the balance begins with recognizing that both masculine and feminine energies are essential to a relationship's stability and depth. A partner who leans into masculine traits may find fulfillment in providing structure, making decisions, and offering protection. They often value autonomy and a clear sense of purpose. When their contributions are acknowledged, they feel respected and empowered. Recognizing their need for independence and leadership strengthens the bond and allows them to support the relationship with confidence.

On the other hand, a partner who embodies more feminine energy may prioritize emotional intimacy, connection, and nurturing. They find joy in cultivating love and creating an atmosphere where empathy and emotional expression are welcomed. For them, relationships are sacred spaces where vulnerability and trust are key. When their desire for closeness is honored, they feel safe and appreciated. Supporting this energy means creating a space where emotions can be expressed openly and where both partners feel emotionally supported.

A healthy balance of these energies enables each partner to contribute their unique qualities, making the relationship strong, harmonious, and adaptable. When masculine energy provides direction and structure, it supports the feminine energy's gift of emotional connection and empathy. Conversely, when feminine energy offers warmth, receptivity, and compassion, it softens the intensity and drive of masculine energy.

Imagine a relationship where one partner takes the lead in planning activities, offering a sense of security and direction, while the other brings joy, spontaneity, and emotional presence to the shared experience. This synergy allows each person to contribute in a way that feels natural and fulfilling. The result is a relationship where both masculine and feminine energies are respected, appreciated, and given space to flourish.

Balancing these energies also involves understanding and honoring personal boundaries. For example, a partner with dominant masculine energy may need space to process challenges independently. Recognizing this need without taking it personally can reduce misunderstandings and offer meaningful support. Similarly, acknowledging a partner's desire for emotional connection without labeling it as "too much" validates their need for closeness. This mutual understanding creates space for both independence and intimacy, helping both partners feel safe, respected, and supported.

The interplay of masculine and feminine energies is not abstract—it shows up in everyday life. From small moments to major decisions, each partner's natural strengths contribute to the relationship's success. Perhaps one partner's feminine energy brings warmth and emotional depth to a late-night conversation, while the other's masculine energy brings clarity and focus to planning the future. When these energies are understood and embraced, even routine interactions become meaningful opportunities for connection and growth.

PART THREE: SETTING THE SAIL

Chapter 1: The Rhythms of Connection

Relationships, like all things in life, are governed by cycles. They ebb and flow, much like the tides of the ocean. There are moments of closeness, where two people feel perfectly in sync, basking in the warmth of connection and shared purpose. Then there are periods of separation—physical, emotional, or even spiritual—where distance, misunderstandings, or life's demands create space between them. These cycles are not signs of failure or dysfunction, but reflections of life's inherent rhythm, which teaches us to embrace both unity and individuality within a relationship.

Understanding the natural cycles of relationships requires us to look beyond our idealized notions of constant harmony. Many of us grew up with stories that equated a "perfect relationship" with unending happiness and unshakable closeness. In reality, relationships are dynamic, living entities. They breathe, stretch, and contract as the individuals within them evolve. The key to navigating these cycles lies in embracing them as opportunities for growth, rather than viewing them as threats to stability.

During phases of closeness, relationships often feel effortless. Communication flows easily, and both partners may find themselves aligned in goals, values, or emotional states. These moments are the lifeblood of a relationship, filling it with joy, intimacy, and connection. They allow for shared experiences that strengthen bonds, whether through laughter, deep conversations, or quiet companionship.

However, even in these seemingly perfect phases, there's a subtle lesson: closeness should not become complacency. It's tempting to settle into these periods without reflection, but this can lead to stagnation. When we assume the good times will always last, we stop nurturing the connection that created them. This is where mindfulness becomes essential. By remaining present and expressing gratitude for closeness, we deepen its impact and prepare ourselves for the inevitable shifts to come.

Then there are periods of separation. Separation is often viewed with fear or apprehension, yet it is as vital to a relationship as closeness. It doesn't always mean physical distance; it can also manifest emotionally, such as when partners feel disconnected due to stress, unresolved conflicts, or personal struggles. At first glance, these periods may seem like failures or signs of trouble. In truth, they often carry the seeds of renewal.

Periods of separation invite introspection. They give each partner space to reconnect with themselves, rediscover their individual needs, and reflect on the relationship without the immediacy of the other person's presence. This distance allows for growth and healing that can strengthen the partnership when closeness returns.

For instance, consider a couple navigating the demands of work and family life. As their schedules pull them in different directions, they may feel a growing emotional distance. Instead of panicking or blaming one another, they can use this time to focus on personal goals or self-care. When they come back together, they do so with fresh energy and a renewed appreciation for each other's presence.

The Danger of Resisting the Cycles

Resistance to these natural cycles often leads to unnecessary pain. When we cling to closeness, we risk suffocating our partner or stifling our own growth. Conversely, when we fear separation, we may act out of desperation, trying to force connection rather than allowing it to return naturally.

Take, for example, a partner who becomes overly controlling during periods of separation. Instead of addressing their fear of losing the connection, they may impose demands or restrictions, unintentionally pushing the other person further away. On the flip side, a partner who denies the value of closeness might emotionally withdraw even during moments of alignment, creating a sense of distance and isolation.

The antidote to resistance is trust: trust in the relationship, trust in your partner, and—most importantly—trust in yourself. Recognizing that cycles are inevitable, and that they are not signs of failure, allows you to navigate them with greater grace and patience.

To move through these cycles effectively, one must first accept that they are part of a relationship's natural rhythm. Acceptance doesn't mean passive resignation—it means acknowledging the reality of change and choosing to respond with intention rather than reactivity.

Self-awareness is a cornerstone of this process. By understanding your own emotions, triggers, and needs, you can meet both closeness and separation with clarity. During a phase of closeness, for instance, self-awareness might help you recognize fears of losing that connection and prevent you from becoming overly dependent. During separation, it can help you discern whether your discomfort stems from the situation itself or from unresolved personal insecurities.

Open communication is equally essential across all phases of a relationship. In periods of closeness, this means expressing appreciation and reinforcing the bond. During separation, it involves sharing your feelings without blame or defensiveness. For example, saying, "I've noticed we haven't spent much time together lately, and I miss you," invites reconnection without assigning fault.

Understanding that nothing in life is permanent—including the phases of your relationship—can offer a deep sense of peace. Rather than fearing the end of a joyful period or dreading the onset of a challenging one, embrace each phase as a teacher. The joy of closeness reminds us of the beauty of connection, while the challenges of separation teach us resilience and self-reliance.

The Role of Emotional Resilience

Building emotional resilience is a lifelong journey, but it is especially crucial in relationships. Resilience enables you to navigate the ups and downs without losing sight of the bigger picture. It helps you remain grounded during periods of separation and fully present during times of closeness.

One way to cultivate resilience is through practices such as mindfulness and meditation. These tools help anchor you in the present moment, rather than allowing fears from the past or anxieties about the future to take over. Journaling can also be a powerful outlet for processing emotions during challenging times, offering both clarity and perspective.

Nature provides profound insight into the cyclical nature of relationships. Consider the changing seasons: spring brings growth and renewal; summer offers warmth and abundance; autumn invites reflection and release; and winter provides rest and introspection. Relationships, too, move through seasons, each carrying its own lessons and gifts.

During the "spring" of a relationship, you may experience excitement and new beginnings. "Summer" might bring deeper connection and shared joy. "Autumn" could involve shedding old patterns or adapting to change, while "winter" offers space for quiet reflection before the cycle begins anew.

By aligning your expectations with these natural rhythms, you can approach your relationship with greater patience, presence, and understanding.

The Law of Rhythm in Relationships

Just as the natural cycles of life shape our relationships, the universal Law of Rhythm governs the emotional and relational dynamics we experience. This principle states that everything in the universe operates in a pattern of rising and falling, ebbing and flowing. In relationships, the Law of Rhythm manifests in the shifts we encounter: moments of harmony and discord, growth and stagnation, connection and withdrawal.

Understanding the Law of Rhythm in relationships can transform how we view change. Often, we resist fluctuations, clinging to the highs and fearing the lows. Yet by making peace with this universal principle, we can find equilibrium amid life's unpredictability and cultivate a deeper, more meaningful connection with our partners.

Relationships are alive with their own pulse, a rhythm created by the interplay of emotions, circumstances, and individual growth. This rhythm ebbs and flows as each partner navigates their inner world while coexisting with another person. At times, the rhythm aligns beautifully, creating a melody of connection and understanding. At other times, it may feel discordant, as personal struggles or external pressures disrupt the harmony.

These fluctuations are natural and inevitable. Like ocean waves rising and falling with the gravitational pull of the moon, relationships respond to forces both seen and unseen. Emotional rhythms may be influenced by stress, personal development, or life transitions such as changes in career, family, or health. Recognizing that these patterns are inherent—not problematic—helps us approach them with curiosity rather than judgment.

One of the most profound lessons the Law of Rhythm offers is the importance of adaptability. In relationships, rigidity often breeds unnecessary conflict. When we expect our partner—or ourselves—to remain static, we set unrealistic expectations that inevitably lead to disappointment. The truth is that both individuals and relationships are constantly evolving.

Consider a couple navigating a major life change, such as the birth of a child or a career transition. The rhythm of their relationship will naturally shift to accommodate new responsibilities, priorities, and emotions. This may cause temporary imbalances, like reduced intimacy or heightened stress. By recognizing this as part of the natural rhythm, they can adapt with patience and grace instead of succumbing to frustration or blame.

Adapting to emotional tides also requires awareness of our own internal rhythms. Each person experiences emotional peaks and valleys, influenced by mood, energy, and external pressures. Understanding your own rhythm, and communicating it to your partner, can help prevent unnecessary misunderstandings. For instance, if you know you tend to feel irritable or withdrawn under stress, sharing that insight allows your partner to offer support rather than misinterpreting your behavior.

Change is the only constant in life, and relationships are no exception. Whether it's the excitement of a new romance or the evolving challenges of a long-term partnership, change requires patience. The Law of Rhythm reminds us that every low point is temporary and will eventually give way to a high point. This perspective fosters resilience, helping us weather difficult times with the assurance that they are part of a larger, ongoing cycle.

Imagine a relationship going through a period of emotional disconnection. One partner may feel frustrated by the lack of closeness, while the other may feel overwhelmed and withdrawn. Without an understanding of rhythm, this situation can spiral into resentment or conflict. But by recognizing that disconnection is a natural phase, not a permanent state, both partners can approach the moment with compassion and patience. Instead of forcing an immediate resolution, they can focus on small, intentional steps to rebuild their connection.

Patience also means allowing yourself and your partner the time and space to grow. Growth rarely happens in a straight line; it often comes in waves, with periods of progress followed by moments of regression or stagnation. Trusting in the natural rhythm of growth can ease the pressure to "fix" things instantly and create space for authentic development.

Every relationship is a dance between two individuals, each with their own unique rhythm. Balancing these rhythms requires attentiveness and compromise. At times, one partner's rhythm may take precedence, such as during a personal crisis or a period of intense focus on career or health. At other times, the relationship's shared rhythm becomes the focus, as both partners align their energy toward a common goal or experience.

The challenge lies in honoring both individual and shared rhythms without losing sight of either. For instance, in a healthy relationship, one partner's need for solitude can coexist with the other's desire for closeness. This balance is achieved through open communication and mutual respect. By acknowledging and validating each other's needs, partners can create a rhythm that accommodates both individuality and connection.

The Law of Rhythm teaches us that the lows in a relationship are not failures, but opportunities for growth. These moments often reveal hidden dynamics or unresolved issues that need attention. While it's natural to resist discomfort, leaning into these challenges can deepen understanding and strengthen the bond.

For example, a recurring argument about finances might point to deeper concerns, such as mismatched values or unmet emotional needs. Rather than seeing the conflict as something to be avoided, a resilient couple can use it as a chance to explore their differences and seek common ground. By addressing the root cause instead of just the symptoms, they can build a stronger foundation for the future.

Just as the lows offer valuable lessons, the highs in a relationship deserve to be celebrated. These moments of connection, joy, and alignment are the rewards of navigating life's rhythms together. Celebrating the highs doesn't mean clinging to them out of fear of their loss. Instead, it means savoring them fully and drawing inspiration from them during more challenging times.

For instance, a couple might create rituals to honor their connection, such as weekly date nights or shared gratitude practices. These rituals reinforce the positive rhythm of the relationship and serve as touchstones for their shared bond.

The Dance of Opposites

The Law of Rhythm is closely linked to the principle of polarity: the idea that opposites exist in harmony. In relationships, this dance of opposites is evident in the interplay between connection and independence, joy and sorrow, giving and receiving. Each element complements and balances the other, creating a dynamic whole.

For example, the independence of each partner allows for personal growth, which in turn enriches their connection. Similarly, moments of sorrow can deepen the capacity for joy, reminding us to fully appreciate the beauty of the highs. Embracing these dualities allows us to experience the full richness of a relationship without clinging to one aspect or rejecting the other.

Ultimately, the Law of Rhythm invites us to trust the natural process of relationships. This trust is not blind optimism, but a grounded faith in life's cycles. It means accepting that change is inevitable and choosing to navigate it with courage and grace.

When we trust the rhythm of a relationship, we free ourselves from the need to control or predict every outcome. Instead, we can focus on being present and responsive, adapting to each moment with openness and curiosity. This trust fosters a sense of security, allowing the relationship to flourish, even amid uncertainty.

Balancing Individuality and Partnership

In the intricate dance of relationships, one of the most delicate challenges is maintaining a balance between individuality and partnership. Relationships often demand a certain level of unity: two people coming together to create a shared life. But in doing so, there's a risk of losing the unique essence that makes each person who they are. Striking the right balance is not just about coexistence but about nurturing a dynamic where self-discovery and authenticity thrive alongside deep connection and shared purpose.

When individuality and partnership are harmoniously balanced, the result is a relationship that uplifts, inspires, and supports the growth of both individuals. This chapter delves into the importance of self-discovery and authenticity in fostering a healthy relational dynamic.

At the core of every healthy relationship is the recognition that each partner is a unique individual. This individuality is shaped by experiences, beliefs, preferences, and dreams, all of which form the essence of a person. Without nurturing this essence, relationships risk becoming stagnant, co-dependent, or emotionally draining.

Being in a relationship does not mean surrendering your identity to the partnership. Instead, it involves bringing your full self into the relationship, offering the richness of your personality, passions, and purpose. When both partners remain true to themselves, they create a vibrant dynamic where differences are celebrated rather than feared, and growth becomes a shared journey.

Self-discovery is an ongoing process that doesn't end when you enter a relationship. In fact, relationships often act as mirrors, reflecting back parts of ourselves we might not otherwise see. While this can be uncomfortable at times, it's also an incredible opportunity for growth.

For example, you may discover new strengths or passions when exposed to your partner's world: perhaps their love for art ignites a latent creativity in you, or their discipline inspires you to pursue your own goals with greater focus. Conversely, a relationship can also highlight areas for growth, such as a tendency to avoid conflict or a struggle with vulnerability.

The key is to embrace these discoveries with curiosity rather than judgment. A willingness to explore your inner world— not just as an individual, but also in the context of your partnership—deepens your understanding of who you are and how you show up in the relationship.

Authenticity is equally important, a bedrock of meaningful relationships. It's about being honest with yourself and your partner about your thoughts, feelings, and needs. Without authenticity, a relationship can feel shallow or performative, with one or both partners hiding their true selves to maintain harmony or avoid rejection.

Being authentic doesn't mean airing every thought or emotion without consideration. It means having the courage to express your truth in a way that is respectful and constructive. For example, if you're feeling overwhelmed by your partner's expectations, authenticity might sound like: "I love being there for you, but I also need some time to recharge."

Authenticity also involves embracing your quirks and imperfections. Too often, people enter relationships trying to present a polished version of themselves, only to struggle later when their true selves emerge. By showing up as you are from the beginning, you create a foundation of trust and acceptance that allows the relationship to grow naturally.

One of the most common challenges in relationships is the tendency to lose yourself in the partnership. This often happens gradually, as you begin to prioritize the relationship over your own needs and desires. While compromise is a natural and healthy part of any relationship, consistently putting your partner's needs above your own can lead to resentment, burnout, or a loss of personal identity.

For example, you might stop pursuing hobbies you love because your partner doesn't share your interests, or you might downplay your career aspirations to avoid conflict. Over time, these small sacrifices can accumulate, leaving you feeling disconnected from your own life.

It's important to remember that taking care of yourself isn't selfish, it's essential. When you prioritize your well-being, you're better equipped to show up fully and authentically for your partner and the relationship. This might mean setting boundaries, carving out time for personal interests, or seeking support when needed.

Healthy relationships don't merely tolerate individuality, they actively encourage it. A strong partnership is one in which both people feel free to explore their passions, pursue their goals, and express their unique identities.

This doesn't mean that partners must always agree or share the same interests. In fact, differences can be a powerful source of growth and inspiration. For instance, one partner's adventurous spirit might encourage the other to step out of their comfort zone, while the other's grounded nature provides stability and perspective.

When both partners are committed to their own growth, the relationship becomes a dynamic space where individuality and togetherness coexist in harmony. This might involve supporting each other's dreams, celebrating one another's achievements, or simply holding space for each other's emotions and experiences.

Balancing individuality and partnership is not a one-time achievement but an ongoing practice. It requires continual communication, mutual respect, and a shared commitment to personal and relational growth. Here are some practical ways to nurture this balance:

1. Communicate openly: Share your thoughts, feelings, and needs regularly, and encourage your partner to do the same.

2. Set boundaries: Identify and express what you need to feel supported, respected, and fulfilled.

3. Pursue personal passions: Make time for hobbies, interests, and goals that bring you joy and a sense of purpose.

4. Celebrate differences: Embrace the unique qualities and perspectives that each partner brings to the relationship.

5. Check in regularly: Periodically evaluate how well the relationship is balancing individuality and partnership, and make adjustments as needed.

When both partners are committed to honoring each other's individuality while nurturing their connection, the result is a relationship that is both dynamic and deeply fulfilling. It's a delicate balance, but one that allows love to flourish in its truest form.

Chapter 2: Boundaries

Defining boundaries and expressing personal needs effectively is an art that requires both self-awareness and relational sensitivity. While many people shy away from these conversations out of fear of conflict or rejection, such discussions are foundational to healthy and fulfilling relationships. Setting boundaries and articulating needs are not about building barriers or creating distance. They pave the way for mutual respect, understanding, and growth.

At the core of this practice is the understanding that boundaries are not selfish but necessary. They serve as reflections of personal values and priorities, offering a clear framework for how you wish to be treated. Without boundaries, relationships can become unbalanced, leading to frustration, resentment, or even burnout.

For example, imagine someone who consistently agrees to every request from their partner, even when it infringes on their own time or well-being. Over time, this dynamic can erode their sense of self and foster unspoken tension that damages the relationship. By defining and communicating boundaries early, you lay the foundation for mutual respect and a healthier, more sustainable dynamic.

Expressing needs is equally crucial. Every person carries a unique set of emotional, physical, and relational requirements that help them feel secure and valued. Yet articulating these needs often feels vulnerable. It can be tempting to assume that your partner should instinctively know what you need, but this expectation is not only unfair, it's also unrealistic. Clear communication is the bridge between intention and understanding, allowing both partners to contribute meaningfully to the relationship.

Consider a situation in which one partner feels neglected because their need for quality time isn't being met. Instead of harboring resentment or waiting for the other person to notice, they might say, "I've been feeling disconnected lately. It would mean a lot to me if we could set aside time this weekend to do something together, just the two of us." This approach not only conveys the need but also invites the partner into a collaborative solution.

The language you use when discussing boundaries and needs can significantly influence the outcome of the conversation. "I statements" are invaluable in this regard, as they allow you to express your feelings without casting blame or triggering defensiveness. For instance, saying, "I feel overwhelmed when I'm left to handle all the household chores alone," is far more effective than, "You never help around the house." The former focuses on your experience and opens the door for dialogue, while the latter is likely to provoke a defensive response.

Moreover, it's essential to be specific and actionable when expressing your needs. Vague or generalized statements can lead to misunderstandings and frustration on both sides. Instead of saying, "I need more support," try framing it as, "I'd appreciate it if you could take care of dinner a couple of nights this week so I can focus on my project." This clarity not only helps your partner understand what you're asking for, but also makes it easier for them to respond positively.

Of course, not every conversation about boundaries or needs will go smoothly. There will be times when your partner may resist or misunderstand your intentions. This resistance often stems from their own fears or insecurities rather than an unwillingness to meet your needs. In such instances, patience and reassurance are key. It can be helpful to reiterate that your intention is not to criticize or reject them, but to strengthen the relationship by ensuring that both of you feel valued and understood.

For example, if your partner reacts negatively to a boundary around personal space, you might say, "I know this might feel unexpected, but I truly believe that having some time for myself will help me show up as a better partner for you. It's not about creating distance. It's about ensuring that I can be the best version of myself in our relationship." Framing your boundaries in this way helps reduce defensiveness and fosters a sense of mutual understanding.

Another important aspect of defining boundaries and needs is learning to say no with kindness and clarity. This can be particularly challenging for people who have been conditioned to prioritize others' needs over their own. However, saying no is not an act of rejection. It's an affirmation of your limits and self-respect. If a request conflicts with your values or well-being, responding with honesty and empathy is vital. For instance, you might say, "I'd love to help you, but I'm already stretched thin this week. Let's figure out another way to get this done."

Consistency is another critical element in maintaining healthy boundaries. Once you've expressed your limits or needs, it's important to uphold them, even when it feels uncomfortable. Letting boundaries slip or failing to follow through on your requests can send mixed signals, making it harder for your partner to understand what you truly need. At the same time, consistency builds trust. When your partner sees that you are committed to respecting yourself, they are more likely to respect you as well.

These practices of boundary-setting and need-expression are not static. Relationships are dynamic, and what works in one phase may need adjustment in another. Regular check-ins can help ensure that both partners remain on the same page and feel supported as the relationship evolves. For example, a couple might revisit their boundaries around work-life balance after one partner starts a demanding new job. Open and honest dialogue allows both individuals to adapt to changes without losing sight of what makes the relationship thrive.

Ultimately, the process of defining boundaries and needs is about creating a partnership where both people feel empowered and respected. It's not about controlling the other person or imposing your will. It's about fostering an environment where both of you can be your authentic selves. By approaching these conversations with empathy, clarity, and a willingness to listen, you lay the groundwork for a relationship that is not only resilient but also deeply fulfilling.

In this context, boundaries and needs become more than just practical tools; they become acts of love. They signal that you care enough about yourself to honor your worth—and enough about your partner to invite them into a relationship built on honesty and mutual respect. While it may take time and effort to master these skills, the reward is a connection that supports and uplifts both individuals, creating a bond that is as empowering as it is enduring.

Reclaiming Agency

Reclaiming agency is about taking control of your life and decisions, ensuring that your choices reflect your true self, values, and aspirations. It involves stepping out of complacency and rejecting behaviors or situations that conflict with who you are and what you stand for. This process isn't easy—it demands courage, self-awareness, and a commitment to living authentically. Yet the rewards are profound: a life that feels purposeful, relationships that align with your values, and a deeper sense of self-worth.

Complacency often sneaks into our lives unnoticed. It begins with small compromises, seemingly harmless at first, but over time, these concessions can accumulate and lead us far from where we intended to be. You might find yourself staying in a job that no longer fulfills you, maintaining friendships that drain rather than uplift you, or tolerating a partner's behavior that diminishes your sense of self. While some level of compromise is necessary in any relationship or situation, the line is crossed when you start sacrificing your core values or ignoring your needs to avoid conflict or preserve the status quo.

Recognizing complacency is the first step in reclaiming your agency. It often manifests as a nagging sense of dissatisfaction or restlessness—a feeling that something isn't quite right. You may feel stuck, as though you're going through the motions without a sense of purpose or direction. These emotions are your internal compass, signaling that something needs to change. The challenge lies in acknowledging these feelings rather than suppressing them, and using them as a catalyst for growth.

Self-worth plays a critical role in breaking free from complacency. When you value yourself, you become less willing to accept situations or behaviors that undermine your well-being. This isn't about arrogance or entitlement; it's about recognizing your inherent worth and refusing to settle for anything that doesn't align with your values and aspirations. Self-worth is the foundation upon which healthy boundaries are built, empowering you to say no to what doesn't serve you and yes to what does.

Embracing self-worth begins with self-reflection. Ask yourself what truly matters: What are your non-negotiables? What kind of relationships and experiences do you want to cultivate? By clarifying your values and priorities, you gain a clearer sense of what aligns with your authentic self, and what doesn't. For instance, if honesty and mutual respect are core values, you may come to realize that a relationship marked by manipulation or dishonesty is no longer acceptable. This awareness can be both liberating and daunting, as it often requires making difficult choices to realign your life with your values.

Once you've identified what matters most, the next step is to take action. Reclaiming agency means actively choosing to live in alignment with your values, rather than passively accepting whatever comes your way. This might involve having honest conversations with your partner about unmet needs, pursuing a job that better reflects your skills and passions, or distancing yourself from friendships that feel one-sided or toxic. These decisions aren't easy, and they may come with temporary discomfort or loss. However, they are essential for building a life that feels authentic and fulfilling.

One of the biggest barriers to reclaiming agency is the fear of the unknown. Complacency often feels safer because it's familiar, even if it's unsatisfying. Stepping into the unknown—whether by ending a relationship, starting a new career path, or asserting a boundary—requires a leap of faith. It's natural to fear making the wrong decision or facing rejection, but these fears shouldn't hold you back. Instead, see them as opportunities for growth. Every step you take toward living authentically strengthens your sense of agency and resilience, making it easier to navigate future challenges.

Another common barrier to reclaiming agency is the tendency to prioritize others' needs and expectations over your own. While caring for others is a virtue, it becomes problematic when it leads to self-neglect. Reclaiming agency involves balancing compassion for others with self-respect. It means recognizing that your needs are just as valid as anyone else's, and that you don't have to sacrifice your well-being to please others. This shift in perspective can be transformative, allowing you to approach relationships and decisions with greater balance and mutual respect.

Reclaiming agency also involves rejecting societal norms and pressures that don't align with your values. Society often imposes expectations about what success, happiness, or love should look like, but these definitions may not resonate with your authentic self. For example, you may feel pressure to stay in a high-paying job because it's seen as a marker of success, even if the work leaves you unfulfilled. Or you might feel obligated to maintain a relationship that looks perfect from the outside, even if it fails to meet your emotional needs. Breaking free from these pressures requires courage, and a willingness to define success and happiness on your own terms.

The process of reclaiming agency is not linear. There will be moments of doubt, setbacks, and second-guessing. You may question whether you're making the right choices or fear that others will judge you for prioritizing your needs. These challenges are a natural part of the journey, and it's important to meet them with self-compassion. Remember that reclaiming agency isn't about perfection, it's about progress. Each small step you take toward living authentically is a victory worth celebrating.

Support from others can play a powerful role in this process. Surround yourself with people who respect your boundaries, encourage your growth, and celebrate your successes. These individuals can serve as sources of strength and inspiration, reminding you of your worth when self-doubt creeps in. At the same time, be mindful of relationships that undermine your sense of agency. If someone consistently dismisses your feelings, invalidates your needs, or pressures you to conform to their expectations, it may be necessary to re-evaluate that relationship.

Ultimately, reclaiming agency is about taking ownership of your life. It means recognizing that you have the power to shape your experiences and make choices that reflect your true self. While you may not control everything—life will always bring challenges and uncertainty—you do have control over how you respond. By aligning your actions with your values and embracing your self-worth, you begin to build a life that feels both meaningful and fulfilling.

The journey to reclaiming agency is deeply personal, and there's no one-size-fits-all approach. What matters most is your commitment to living authentically and honoring your worth. This path may require patience, perseverance, and a willingness to sit with discomfort, but the rewards are immeasurable. By rejecting complacency and embracing your agency, you open the door to a life filled with purpose, connection, and joy—a life that truly reflects who you are.

Chapter 3: Transformative Communication

Giving sincere appreciation is an art that transforms relationships. It isn't just about offering compliments or casually saying "thank you"; it's about forging a genuine connection by recognizing another person's efforts, qualities, and contributions. When expressed authentically, appreciation becomes a powerful bridge that deepens trust and strengthens emotional bonds.

In any relationship, there's an inherent need to feel valued. Whether it's a partner, friend, family member, or colleague, everyone seeks acknowledgment for who they are and what they bring to the table. Yet this need often goes unnoticed: drowned out by routine, stress, or the assumption that our appreciation is understood. The truth is, unspoken gratitude often leaves a void, creating a subtle but persistent distance.

To bridge that gap, appreciation must become an intentional practice. It's not simply about saying the right words, it's about recognizing specific actions or qualities that merit acknowledgment. For instance, rather than offering a generic compliment like, "You're amazing," it's far more impactful to say, "I noticed how you handled that difficult situation with so much patience and kindness—it really impressed me." This kind of expression highlights not just the action, but the unique character behind it, making the appreciation feel personal and heartfelt.

It's also important to understand that appreciation isn't limited to grand gestures or major accomplishments. Often, the most profound connections arise from recognizing small, everyday efforts that might otherwise go unnoticed. A partner who prepares a meal after a long day, a friend who checks in with a thoughtful message, or a colleague who takes on extra work to lighten the load: these seemingly minor acts form the foundation of meaningful relationships. By acknowledging these moments, we affirm that no act of kindness is too small to matter.

Sincerity is the heart of true appreciation. Empty or forced compliments can backfire, creating feelings of mistrust or disconnection. People instinctively sense when words lack authenticity. To ensure appreciation resonates, it must come from a genuine place. This means slowing down, paying attention, and reflecting on what we truly value in others. It's about moving beyond the surface to recognize how their actions affect us personally.

Nonverbal cues also play a powerful role in conveying appreciation. A warm smile, a gentle touch, or sustained eye contact can communicate gratitude in ways words sometimes cannot. These gestures foster an atmosphere of warmth and acknowledgment, reinforcing the sincerity of verbal expressions. For example, a simple pat on the shoulder accompanied by a heartfelt, "You did such a great job," can leave a lasting impression.

Timing is another powerful element in expressing appreciation. While it's never too late to acknowledge someone's efforts, timely gratitude carries special weight. Expressing it in the moment—or shortly after—makes the recognition feel immediate and meaningful. Waiting too long can dull the impact, as the connection to the original act may fade.

The act of giving sincere appreciation isn't just beneficial for the recipient—it transforms the giver as well. When we focus on recognizing the good in others, it naturally shifts our perspective. We begin to see the world through a lens of positivity, which can uplift our mood and foster a deeper sense of gratitude in daily life. This creates a powerful feedback loop: as we appreciate others, we become more attuned to the kindness and efforts around us, making it easier to continue the cycle.

In relationships, this practice helps build a culture of mutual respect and validation. When both people feel seen and valued, it fosters a sense of safety and connection that strengthens the bond over time. Appreciation becomes a form of emotional nourishment, allowing the relationship to thrive, even during challenging moments.

Importantly, how we express appreciation should align with what resonates most with the other person. Some people value words of affirmation, while others respond more deeply to acts of service, quality time, or physical touch. Paying attention to these preferences ensures that our gratitude has the intended impact. For instance, a partner might cherish a simple, heartfelt note left on the kitchen counter, while a colleague may appreciate public recognition during a team meeting.

It's also worth remembering that appreciation doesn't always require words. Sometimes, actions speak louder. Offering to take on a task for someone who's overwhelmed, surprising a loved one with their favorite treat, or simply being fully present during a conversation can serve as powerful demonstrations of gratitude. These gestures show that we're attentive and that we care, often more effectively than spoken compliments.

In practicing appreciation, it's vital to avoid transactional thinking. Genuine gratitude isn't about expecting something in return or keeping score. When appreciation is given with strings attached, it loses its authenticity and may even harm the relationship. True appreciation is offered freely, with the understanding that the act itself deepens connection and trust.

As we cultivate this habit, we also begin to notice the beauty in imperfection. No one is perfect, and every relationship has its flaws. Yet by focusing on the positive qualities of those we care about, we create an environment where growth and acceptance can flourish. This doesn't mean ignoring concerns, but rather choosing to emphasize the good while addressing challenges with empathy and care.

In many ways, giving sincere appreciation is a practice of mindfulness. It calls us to be present, to truly see and value the people in our lives, and to express that recognition in meaningful ways. It's a simple yet profound act that, when practiced consistently, has the power to transform not just our relationships, but our entire outlook on life.

Conflict as a Growth Opportunity

Conflict is an inevitable part of every relationship. Whether in a romantic partnership, a friendship, or the workplace, disagreements and misunderstandings are bound to arise. However, rather than viewing conflict as a source of division, we can choose to see it as an opportunity for growth, both individually and collectively. The way we approach conflict ultimately determines whether it strengthens or weakens the relationship.

At its core, conflict often stems from differences, whether in opinions, values, expectations, or emotional processing. These differences are natural. They reflect the uniqueness of each individual and the diverse ways in which we perceive and experience the world. Conflict, therefore, is not inherently damaging to relationships; it is our response to it that makes all the difference.

In many relationships, the instinct is to avoid conflict: to smooth things over or give in for the sake of peace. Yet avoidance often means missing out on valuable opportunities to deepen our understanding of ourselves and others. Unresolved conflicts tend to simmer beneath the surface, creating tension that can slowly erode trust and connection. Conversely, when handled with care and intention, conflict can lead to greater intimacy, understanding, and emotional resilience.

The first step in transforming conflict into an opportunity for growth is to shift our perspective. Instead of seeing a disagreement as something negative or threatening, we can reframe it as a natural—and even necessary—part of the relational process. Disagreements provide a chance to learn about another person's values, needs, and boundaries, while also clarifying our own. In this way, conflict becomes a pathway to self-discovery and mutual insight.

One of the most critical components of constructive conflict resolution is communication. Rather than resorting to blame or defensiveness, effective communication emphasizes expressing our feelings and needs in ways that foster understanding. This means taking responsibility for our own emotions and experiences, rather than projecting them onto others. For example, instead of saying, "You always make me feel unheard," we might say, "I feel unheard when I'm speaking and don't receive a response." This approach shifts the focus from accusing the other person to sharing our internal experience—making it easier for the other person to hear us without becoming defensive.

Equally important is learning to listen actively. In the heat of disagreement, it's easy to become consumed by our own thoughts and feelings. But active listening requires us to quiet those internal dialogues and fully engage with what the other person is expressing. It means paying attention not only to their words, but also to their tone, body language, and emotional cues. When we listen with empathy and presence, we create space for genuine understanding, which in turn fosters deeper connection.

It's important to remember that conflict doesn't have to be a zero-sum game. Both people in a disagreement don't need to "win" for the relationship to benefit. In fact, the most successful relationships are often those where both individuals are willing to compromise and seek common ground. Compromise doesn't mean abandoning your values or needs—it means finding a way to meet in the middle, allowing both people to feel heard, respected, and valued. This process of give-and-take fosters trust and strengthens the bond between individuals, demonstrating a shared commitment to mutual understanding.

Conflict also presents an opportunity for vulnerability. When we are open and honest about our feelings, we allow the other person to see us more clearly—our fears, needs, and struggles. This kind of vulnerability deepens connection, inviting the other person to respond with empathy and care. Though vulnerability can feel uncomfortable—especially when emotions run high—it is through this openness that we truly grow together. By showing up as our authentic selves in the midst of conflict, we create a space for mutual learning and emotional evolution.

Moreover, conflict offers a valuable lens for personal and relational growth by revealing underlying patterns and behaviors that may need to change. Often, disagreements are rooted in deeper issues: unmet needs, miscommunications, or unresolved past experiences. By examining the root causes of conflict, we can uncover recurring patterns that may no longer serve the relationship, such as avoiding confrontation, suppressing emotions, or fearing vulnerability. Recognizing and addressing these dynamics can catalyze meaningful growth and healing.

In relationships, growth often comes through discomfort. It's easy to remain in familiar habits, even when they're unhelpful. And while it may be tempting to avoid conflict for the sake of short-term peace, true growth demands that we lean into discomfort and confront challenges directly. When we approach conflict with curiosity and openness, we create an environment where both people have the opportunity to evolve together.

Conflict also acts as a mirror, reflecting aspects of ourselves we may not fully recognize. During disagreements, we often project our own insecurities, fears, or frustrations onto the other person. But conflict invites introspection. What are we bringing into this situation? Are we communicating clearly? Are we holding on to outdated patterns or assumptions? Honest reflection allows us to take responsibility for our role in the conflict and to grow from the experience, not just as individuals, but as partners in a shared journey.

Ultimately, the key to transforming conflict into a growth opportunity is a commitment to mutual respect. Conflict is a natural part of any relationship, but how we handle it determines the trajectory of that relationship. When both people are willing to engage with one another in an open, honest, and compassionate way, conflict becomes a catalyst for change, learning, and deeper connection.

It's also important to remember that not every conflict will be resolved immediately, and that's okay. Some disagreements take time to process. The goal isn't to "win" the argument, but to understand each other's perspectives and find a way to move forward together. Sometimes, this means giving each other space to process emotions before returning to the conversation. Other times, it may involve accepting that certain differences will always exist and learning to navigate them with mutual respect and care.

Over time, as we practice managing conflict in healthy, constructive ways, we develop stronger conflict resolution skills. We become more adept at regulating our emotions, listening actively, and expressing ourselves clearly. These skills not only enhance the quality of our relationships, but also contribute to our overall emotional intelligence, making us more resilient in the face of life's inevitable challenges.

In conclusion, conflict is not something to fear or avoid. Rather, it is an opportunity to grow together—to learn more about ourselves and each other—and to build stronger, more resilient relationships. By approaching conflict with an open mind, a compassionate heart, and a willingness to engage in honest communication, we can transform even the most difficult disagreements into stepping stones toward deeper connection and shared growth.

Chapter 4: The Power of Shared Purpose

In the journey of a relationship, the most profound connections are often those built on a shared sense of purpose. While passion and attraction may ignite the initial spark, it is the deeper alignment of values, goals, and vision that sustains the flame. A shared purpose transcends immediate needs or desires, forging a bond capable of withstanding the test of time. It becomes a guiding force through both triumphs and trials, helping couples navigate life's complexities with a unified sense of direction.

Relationships that thrive are those in which both partners are committed to something greater than themselves. This shared purpose can take many forms: a vision for the future, common ambitions, or a dedication to mutual growth. Whatever shape it takes, when partners align around a higher purpose, it elevates their connection. It becomes the glue that holds them together, particularly during moments of hardship or conflict. Challenges are no longer threats. They become opportunities to deepen the bond and grow together.

A relationship rooted in shared purpose adds depth to even the most ordinary interactions. It lends significance to daily moments and provides a context for the decisions each partner makes. Whether it's how they spend their time, manage their finances, or raise their children, a shared purpose serves as a framework for these choices. This sense of unity fosters mutual respect, deeper understanding, and collaborative decision-making.

However, arriving at a shared purpose does not happen overnight. It requires open, honest conversations about each person's desires, dreams, and expectations. It involves understanding what truly matters to each partner and weaving those values into the fabric of the relationship. This journey of discovery takes time, and it demands patience and empathy. Yet once a shared vision emerges, it becomes a powerful tool for cultivating harmony and longevity.

A shared purpose also provides clarity. Relationships can be tested by external pressures: career demands, financial stress, or social expectations. Without a clear sense of direction, couples may drift apart or lose sight of what they truly want. In these moments, a shared purpose acts as an anchor, offering stability and reminding partners of what they are striving for together. It helps them remain focused on the bigger picture rather than being consumed by temporary difficulties.

Moreover, a shared purpose fosters resilience. Life is unpredictable, and every couple will face storms: personal crises, family struggles, financial setbacks. But when a relationship is built on a strong foundation of shared intent, it is more likely to endure. Partners who are equally invested in a larger goal find strength in solidarity. They are reminded that they are not alone and that they are working together toward something meaningful. This shared commitment becomes a source of support, perseverance, and enduring love.

The Balance Between Independence and Togetherness

While a shared purpose provides a strong foundation for a relationship, it's equally important to maintain a balance between personal autonomy and the emotional connection that binds partners together. In healthy relationships, each individual should be able to retain their identity while also nurturing the shared bond. This balance is delicate, requiring both partners to support one another's personal growth without losing sight of their collective journey.

Personal autonomy is essential to a fulfilling partnership. When individuals are free to pursue their passions, dreams, and personal goals, they bring renewed energy and vitality into the relationship. This independence fosters self-worth and confidence, qualities that are often deeply attractive to a partner. Moreover, it helps prevent feelings of suffocation or over-dependence, ensuring that both people feel whole and fulfilled on their own.

However, independence should not come at the expense of emotional intimacy. Relationships flourish when both partners feel deeply connected and supported. While giving each other space to grow is important, investing in the emotional bond is equally vital. This includes prioritizing shared experiences, being present in times of need, and nurturing the connection built on mutual purpose. Emotional intimacy strengthens trust and security, enabling both partners to feel seen, safe, and valued.

In practice, maintaining this balance requires intentional communication. Couples must regularly check in with one another to ensure their individual goals are respected while remaining emotionally attuned. It's about discovering the "sweet spot" where each person can thrive independently while continuing to grow together. For instance, one partner might be pursuing a demanding career, while the other is focused on education or creative pursuits. As long as both respect each other's time and space—and continue to prioritize their connection—they can sustain a healthy equilibrium between independence and togetherness.

Emotional Safety as the Foundation of Trust

At the heart of every strong relationship lies trust. Trust is the bedrock of emotional intimacy, and it cannot exist without emotional safety. Emotional safety is the sense of security that allows individuals to express their true selves without fear of judgment, ridicule, or rejection. It is the environment in which vulnerability thrives, where each partner feels fully supported and accepted for who they are.

Creating emotional safety requires openness, honesty, and mutual respect. Partners must be willing to listen deeply to each other's thoughts, feelings, and concerns, without becoming defensive or dismissive. It's about fostering a space where both individuals feel genuinely heard and understood, even in moments of disagreement. Emotional safety nurtures psychological safety, making it possible for both people to share authentically, knowing their emotions and perspectives will be valued.

When emotional safety is present, trust naturally follows. Trust cannot be demanded or rushed—it is cultivated over time through consistent actions that convey care, empathy, and dependability. It's built in the small moments: a kind word, a listening ear, the reliability of showing up for one another. These daily acts of presence and respect accumulate, gradually forming a strong foundation. Once trust is established, it becomes the solid ground upon which love deepens and the relationship continues to grow.

Breaking Cycles of Conflict: Moving from Reactive to Proactive Engagement

Every relationship experiences conflict. Disagreements are a natural part of any partnership, but how couples handle them can make or break the relationship. In many cases, conflict becomes a destructive cycle of defensiveness, blame, and anger. These reactive patterns prevent both partners from truly hearing one another and from addressing the underlying issues. Over time, such dynamics can erode trust and create emotional distance.

Shifting from reactive conflict to proactive engagement requires a change in mindset. Rather than viewing conflict as a threat or a sign of failure, couples can begin to see disagreements as opportunities for growth and deeper understanding. Approaching conflict with curiosity and openness allows partners to explore each other's perspectives and strengthen their connection. Proactive engagement involves taking ownership of one's emotions and behavior, rather than projecting blame. It means working together to find solutions that meet both partners' needs, rather than getting trapped in cycles of hurt and resentment.

This shift demands emotional maturity and a commitment to healthy communication. Couples who practice active listening, empathy, and collaboration can transform conflict into a tool for greater intimacy. By doing so, they build a more resilient relationship, one grounded in mutual respect, self-awareness, and a shared commitment to growth.

Energetic Synchronization: Understanding the Invisible Dynamics of Relationships

In every relationship, invisible forces are at play. These forces—the emotional energies, intentions, and beliefs that each partner brings—interact in ways that shape the relationship's overall dynamic. Understanding and harmonizing these energies is key to creating a connection that is not only functional but also deeply fulfilling.

Energetic synchronization is the process of becoming attuned to each other's emotional states, needs, and desires. It's about recognizing the natural ebb and flow of feelings and learning how to support one another without overpowering or neglecting each other. This attunement requires a level of awareness that goes beyond words. It involves picking up on nonverbal cues such as body language, tone of voice, and facial expressions, as well as understanding the emotions that underlie those signals.

When partners are energetically synchronized, they cultivate a seamless flow of communication and support. The relationship feels more effortless, as both individuals are in tune with each other's rhythms and can navigate life's challenges as a unified team. Energetic synchronization may be subtle, but its impact is profound: it strengthens emotional connection and helps couples move through the world with a sense of cohesion and harmony.

The Transformative Power of Forgiveness and Release

No relationship is without its challenges, and inevitably, partners will hurt each other. Whether through careless words, broken promises, or unmet expectations, forgiveness is essential for healing and moving forward. Forgiveness is not about excusing harmful behavior or pretending the pain didn't occur. It's about releasing the grip of the past and creating space for a more hopeful and constructive future.

Equally important is self-forgiveness. Many people hold onto their own mistakes, burdened by guilt or the belief that they are undeserving of grace. But true healing begins within. By forgiving ourselves, we open the door to growth and approach our partners with greater compassion and empathy. Letting go of resentment is not a single act; it's an ongoing process of lightening the emotional load and inviting in healthier dynamics.

When forgiveness is embraced within a relationship, it generates a profound sense of renewal. It clears the emotional slate, allowing both partners to move forward unencumbered by old wounds. This process cultivates deeper trust, empathy, and emotional intimacy, laying the groundwork for a stronger and more connected future.

From Love to Partnership: Evolving from Romantic Love to a Balanced Partnership

As relationships mature, so does the nature of love. The thrill of early infatuation gradually gives way to a deeper, more sustainable form of love, one grounded in mutual respect, shared responsibility, and emotional maturity. This evolution, while natural, can be challenging, as couples navigate shifting roles, new expectations, and growing commitments. Yet it is through this transition that relationships gain depth and resilience.

This shift calls for ongoing communication and a willingness to adapt. Partners must continually re-evaluate and renegotiate their responsibilities, ensuring that both individuals feel seen, valued, and supported. Through this mutual effort, they establish a true partnership, one built on equality, cooperation, and shared purpose.

Sustaining Trust: Daily Practices That Reinforce Connection

At the heart of a healthy, thriving relationship lies consistent, intentional practice. Trust, intimacy, and connection are not static. They must be nurtured daily. Small yet meaningful actions, such as regular emotional check-ins, expressing gratitude, and upholding clear boundaries, play a crucial role in reinforcing the foundation of the relationship.

By integrating these habits into their everyday lives, couples foster a bond that is both sustainable and resilient, capable of weathering life's inevitable challenges with grace and unity.

When couples nurture trust, uphold emotional safety, and honor one another's individuality, they create a relationship that is not only deeply fulfilling but enduring. Relationships grounded in shared purpose, balanced in independence and togetherness, and guided by forgiveness and open communication possess the power to last a lifetime.

Charting the Course for Lasting Relationships

The journey of relationships is both a deeply personal and universal experience. This book has explored the complexities of human connection, offering insights and tools to help navigate challenges and embrace the beauty of partnership. Now, as we conclude, it's time to bring these ideas together, reflect on their significance, and consider how they can be implemented in daily life. Relationships are not static; they require ongoing attention, effort, and intentionality. This afterword serves as both a summary and a guide, designed to encourage you to take the principles explored here and put them into practice in ways that feel authentic and meaningful.

At the heart of every strong relationship is self-awareness. Before we can truly connect with another person, we must understand ourselves. This involves more than just knowing our likes and dislikes. It's about recognizing our values, emotional triggers, strengths, and areas for growth. Building self-awareness requires both reflection and honesty. Taking time each day to assess how you feel and why can be incredibly helpful. Journaling is a powerful tool for this, as are conversations with trusted friends or professionals who can offer valuable outside perspectives. Growth begins within. The more we understand ourselves, the more we can bring to our relationships.

Once we know ourselves, the next step is to align with a shared purpose in our partnerships. Thriving relationships are often those in which both individuals look beyond personal needs to pursue common goals. These goals could be as simple as creating a peaceful home or as ambitious as building a family or contributing to the community. What matters is the process of discovery—talking openly with your partner about your dreams, values, and aspirations. These conversations not only deepen mutual understanding but also strengthen bonds by fostering a sense of unity. The world will always present challenges, but a couple united by a shared purpose will be better equipped to weather any storm.

While unity is essential, it's equally important to honor individuality within a relationship. Each partner brings a unique identity, shaped by personal experiences, interests, and aspirations. Maintaining individuality doesn't mean distancing oneself from the relationship; rather, it means creating space for both people to grow. A healthy balance between independence and togetherness can be achieved by respecting each other's boundaries, celebrating individual achievements, and encouraging personal passions. When both partners thrive as individuals, the relationship becomes a space of mutual inspiration and support.

Another cornerstone of lasting partnerships is emotional safety. This allows us to be vulnerable—to share our true selves without fear of judgment or rejection. Emotional safety is cultivated through consistent, caring actions: listening without interrupting, offering reassurance in moments of doubt, and responding with kindness rather than criticism. When we create a safe environment, trust grows naturally. Partners can then navigate conflict with openness and curiosity, viewing disagreements not as threats but as opportunities to learn and grow together.

Conflict, though uncomfortable, is a natural part of any relationship. What matters most is not the presence of conflict, but how it is handled. Reactive responses—such as defensiveness or blame—tend to escalate tension, while proactive engagement fosters understanding. When disagreements arise, it's helpful to pause and reflect before responding. Approaching the conversation with a sincere desire to understand your partner's perspective can shift the dynamic from confrontation to collaboration. Instead of asking, "How can I prove my point?" try asking, "How can we solve this together?" This mindset encourages teamwork and builds resilience in the face of challenges.

Forgiveness is another vital ingredient in sustaining relationships. No partnership is perfect, and mistakes are inevitable. Forgiveness is not about condoning hurtful behavior but about releasing resentment and making space for healing. It's a process that requires patience and empathy. When hurt arises, it's important to acknowledge it openly, express how it affected you, and work together to rebuild trust. Holding onto grudges only perpetuates pain, while forgiveness allows both partners to move forward with renewed clarity and compassion.

As relationships evolve, so do the roles we play within them. The excitement of initial romance often gives way to a deeper partnership rooted in mutual respect and shared responsibility. This transition is natural and should be embraced as an opportunity to strengthen the connection. It requires ongoing communication and a willingness to adapt. Partners must regularly check in with each other: discussing what's working, what's not, and how they can continue to grow together. This willingness to adjust ensures that the relationship remains dynamic and fulfilling.

Small, daily actions are often the most powerful in sustaining trust and connection over time. Consistent communication, expressions of gratitude, and moments of shared joy build a strong foundation. Simple gestures—like a thoughtful note, a kind word, or a shared meal—remind your partner that they are valued and loved. These practical steps may seem small, but their cumulative impact is profound. They create a sense of stability and warmth that anchors the relationship even during difficult times.

Begin with Self-Awareness

Every relationship starts with the individual. To foster a healthy partnership, you must first know yourself: your values, triggers, strengths, and areas for growth. Self-awareness is the foundation upon which authentic connections are built.

Practical Steps:

1. Journal Regularly: Dedicate 10–15 minutes each day to reflect on your emotions, experiences, and interactions

with others. Identify recurring patterns and assess how they align with your values.

2. Seek Feedback: Ask trusted friends or mentors to share their perceptions of you. Their insights can reveal blind spots and help you grow.

3. Invest in Personal Growth: Whether through therapy, self-help books, or courses, commit to becoming the best version of yourself. The stronger your sense of self, the more you can bring to the relationship.

Establish a Shared Purpose

As discussed, a shared sense of purpose binds relationships in ways that transcend the everyday. This purpose acts as a compass, guiding decisions and offering direction during turbulent times.

Practical Steps:

1. Define Your Vision Together: Sit down with your partner and discuss your goals for the future, both as individuals and as a couple. Write down your shared

aspirations, whether they involve building a family, contributing to your community, or pursuing a particular lifestyle.

2. Create Rituals: Establish shared practices that align with your purpose. For instance, if health is a mutual goal, schedule weekly workout sessions together or prepare nutritious meals as a team.

3. Revisit and Adjust: Life changes, and so do priorities. Periodically review your shared purpose to ensure it remains relevant and meaningful.

Balance Independence and Togetherness

One of the most delicate dynamics in relationships is balancing personal autonomy with emotional intimacy. Both are essential for a thriving partnership.

1. Schedule "Me Time": Encourage each other to pursue individual hobbies, friendships, and interests. Independence fosters growth and helps prevent resentment.

2. Set Boundaries: Discuss what independence looks like for each of you. For instance, one partner may need solitude to recharge, while the other may thrive on frequent social interaction. Respect these differences.

3. Celebrate Each Other's Wins: When your partner achieves a personal goal, celebrate their success as if it were your own. This reinforces the idea that individual growth strengthens the relationship.

Cultivate Emotional Safety

Trust is the backbone of any relationship, and emotional safety is what allows trust to flourish. Partners who feel emotionally secure are more likely to communicate openly, resolve conflicts effectively, and deepen their connection.

1. Listen Actively: When your partner speaks, give them your full attention. Avoid interrupting or planning your response while they're talking. Focus instead on understanding their perspective.

2. Express Appreciation: Regularly acknowledge your partner's efforts, whether big or small. A simple "thank you" can go a long way in making someone feel valued.

3. Create a Safe Space for Vulnerability: Respond to your partner's fears or mistakes with compassion rather than judgment. Let them know it's okay to be imperfect.

Navigate Conflict with Intention

Conflict is inevitable, but it doesn't have to be destructive. When approached with intention and care, disagreements can actually strengthen a relationship.

1. Pause Before Reacting: In the heat of an argument, take a moment to breathe and collect your thoughts. This prevents reactive behaviors like yelling or blaming.

2. Use "I" Statements: Frame concerns in terms of your own feelings rather than accusing your partner. For example, say, "I feel hurt when you don't call," instead of, "You never think about me."

3. Focus on Solutions: Rather than dwelling on the problem, work together to find a resolution that satisfies both parties. This shifts the dynamic from adversarial to collaborative.

Embrace the Power of Forgiveness

No relationship is without mistakes. Forgiveness is not about excusing hurtful behavior but about releasing the emotional weight of resentment. It paves the way for healing and renewal.

1. Acknowledge the Hurt: Before forgiveness can occur, both partners must recognize the impact of the offense. This involves honest conversations and active listening.

2. Practice Empathy: Try to understand your partner's perspective, even if you don't agree with their actions. Empathy fosters compassion and reduces judgment.

3. Let Go of the Grudge: Holding onto anger only harms you in the long run. Focus on the future rather than replaying the past.

Adapt to the Evolution of Love

Romantic relationships evolve organically. The passionate infatuation of the early days often transitions into a deeper, steadier form of love rooted in partnership and mutual respect.

1. Celebrate Milestones: Acknowledge your journey as a couple by celebrating anniversaries, achievements, and other significant moments. This reinforces the bond you've built.

2. Stay Curious: Even after years together, continue to learn about your partner. Ask questions about their dreams, fears, and evolving interests.

3. Redefine Roles: As life circumstances change, so do the roles you play in each other's lives. Be willing to renegotiate responsibilities to maintain balance and harmony.

Foster Daily Connection

Strong relationships are built on consistent effort. It's the small, everyday actions that ultimately determine the health of a partnership.

1. Check In Daily: Make it a habit to ask your partner how their day went, and genuinely listen to their response. These moments of connection create a sense of closeness.

2. Express Gratitude: Regularly remind your partner of what you appreciate about them. Gratitude nurtures positivity and reinforces emotional bonds.

3. Prioritize Quality Time: In our busy lives, it's easy to let time together slip through the cracks. Schedule regular date nights or shared activities to keep the spark alive.

As we reflect on the themes of this book, it becomes clear that the principles of self-awareness, shared purpose, emotional safety, and mutual respect are not just abstract ideas. They are actionable strategies. The key to implementing them lies in intention. Life's demands can easily divert our attention from our relationships, but maintaining connection requires a conscious choice. By dedicating time and energy to the people we love, we affirm their importance in our lives.

Building a meaningful relationship is an ongoing journey, not a final destination. There will be moments of joy and moments of struggle, but each experience offers a chance for growth. The beauty of relationships lies in their ability to teach us about ourselves and the world around us. Through connection, we cultivate empathy, resilience, and the transformative power of love.

As you move forward, remember that the tools and insights shared in this book are just the beginning. The true work of building a strong relationship happens in the everyday moments: in the way you listen, the way you support, and the way you show up for each other. Approach your partnership with curiosity, humility, and a willingness to grow. By doing so, you can create a bond that not only endures but thrives, bringing lasting fulfillment and joy to both your lives.

May this book inspire you to embrace the journey of relationships with an open heart and a determined spirit. The path may not always be easy, but it is undoubtedly one of the most rewarding paths you can take. Let love be your guide, and let your actions reflect the depth of your commitment to those you hold dear. Through intentionality, compassion, and consistent effort, you can create relationships that are not only lasting but deeply enriching, allowing you to experience the true beauty of connection.